Prophets of the Fourth Estate

Prophets of the Fourth Estate

Broadsides by Press Critics of the Progressive Era

Amy Reynolds & Gary R. Hicks

Litwin Books

Los Angeles, CA

Published in January 2012 by Litwin Books, LLC

Litwin Books
PO Box 25322
Los Angeles, CA 90025

http://litwinbooks.com/

Printed on acid-free and sustainably-sourced paper.

Library of Congress Cataloging-in-Publication Data

Reynolds, Amy, 1967–
Prophets of the fourth estate : broadsides by press critics of the progressive
era / Amy Reynolds & Gary R. Hicks.
    p. cm.
Summary: "An historical look at criticism of the mainstream press during
the Progressive Era, consisting of original articles from the time and context-
providing essays"--Provided by publisher.
   Includes bibliographical references and index.
   ISBN 978-0-9802004-6-1 (alk. paper)
1. Journalism--Social aspects--United States--History--20th century.   2. Jour-
nalism--Political aspects--United States--History--20th century.   3. Press and
politics--United States--History--20th century.   4. Social problems--Press
coverage--United States.   5. Progressivism (United States politics)--History-
-20th century. I. Reynolds, Amy, 1967– II. Hicks, Gary R., 1962– III. Title.
PN4888.S6R49 2012
071'.309041--dc22
                                2011014712

For our friend and mentor Bob Jensen

A.R. & G.R.H.

Table of Contents

Foreword

Robert Jensen[1]
December 2010

The managers of commercial news organizations in the United States love to proclaim their independence from the corporate suits who sign their paychecks. Extolling the unbreachable "firewall" between the journalistic and the business sides of the operation, these editors and news directors wax eloquent about their ability to pursue any story without interference from the corporate front office.

"No one from corporate headquarters has ever called me to tell me what to run in my paper," one editor (let's call him Joe) told me proudly after hearing my critique of the overwhelmingly commercial news media system in the United States.

I asked Joe if it were possible that he simply had internalized the value system of the folks who run the corporation (and, by extension, the folks who run the world), and therefore they never needed to give him direct instructions.

He rejected that, reasserting his independence from any force outside his newsroom. I countered:

"Let's say, for the purposes of discussion, that you and I were equally capable journalists in terms of professional skills, and we were both reasonable candidates for the job of editor-in-chief that you hold. If we had both applied for the job, do you think your corporate bosses would have ever considered me for the position given my politics? Would I, for even a second, have been seen by them to be a viable candidate for the job?"

1   Robert Jensen is a Professor in the School of Journalism at the University of Texas at Austin. In addition to teaching and research, Jensen writes for popular media, both alternative and mainstream. His opinion and analytic pieces on such subjects as foreign policy, politics, and race have appeared in papers and on websites around the world.

Joe's politics are pretty conventional, well within the range of mainstream Republicans and Democrats – he supports big business and U.S. supremacy in global politics and economics. In other words, he's a capitalist and imperialist. I am on the political left, anti-capitalist and critical of the U.S. empire. On some political issues, Joe and I would agree, but we diverge sharply on the core questions of the nature of the economy and foreign policy.

Joe pondered my question and conceded that I was right, that his bosses would never hire someone with my politics, no matter how qualified, to run one of their newspapers. The conversation trailed off, and we parted without resolving our differences.

I would like to think my critique at least got Joe to question his platitudes, but I never saw any evidence of that. In his subsequent writing and public comments that I read and heard, Joe continued to assert that a news media system dominated by for-profit corporations was the best way to produce the critical, independent journalism that citizens in a democracy needed. After he retired from the paper, he signed on as a "senior adviser" with a high-powered lobbying/public relations firm, apparently without a sense of irony, or shame.

The collapse of mainstream journalism's business model has given news managers less time to pontificate as they scramble to figure out how to stay afloat, but the smug, self-satisfied attitude hasn't changed much.

As a former journalist, I certainly understood Joe's position. When I was a working reporter and editor, I would have asserted my journalistic independence in similar fashion, a viewpoint that reflected the dominant assumptions of newsroom culture. We saw ourselves as non-ideological and uncontrolled. We knew there were owners and bosses whose political views clearly were not radical, and we knew we worked in a larger ideological system. But we working journalists were convinced that we were not constrained.

It was not until I got some critical distance from the daily grind of journalism that I learned there were compelling analyses of the news media that questioned those assumptions I had taken for granted. That media criticism, which had taken off in the 1970s on the heels of the progressive and radical social movements of the '60s, was a rich source of new insights for me, first as a graduate student and later as a professor.

But that was only part of my education about the political economy of journalism. As is so often the case, I needed to look to the past to better understand the present. While I had immersed myself in contemporary criticism, I had been slow to look at history, and turning to the critiques of journalism from the progressive/populist era of the early 20th century proved fruitful. Early critics of the commercial news media were pointing out the ways that media owners' interest in profit undermined journalists' desire to serve the public interest. Owners and managers are interested in news that serves the bottom line, while journalists are supposed to be pursuing news that serves democracy.

The writings collected and analyzed in this volume provide that historical context. This material is important for the ways it reminds us of a simple truth: An overwhelmingly commercial, for-profit media system based on advertising will never adequately serve citizens in a democracy. But while history helps us recognize simple truths, it does not lead to simplistic predictions – we study history not only to identify the continuities, but also to help us understand the effects of the inevitable changes in institutions and systems.

Indeed, news media and society as a whole have changed over the century. Most obvious are the recent economic changes that have undermined the business model of commercial media. Newspapers and broadcast television stations were wildly profitable through the 20th century, which subsidized an annoying cockiness on the part of owners, managers, and working journalists. Competition from digital media has wiped that smug smile off the face of mainstream journalism, leaving everyone scrambling to come up with a new model. But to focus only on the recent economic crisis would be to miss other trends in the past century that are at least as important.

Reporters who were once members of the working class have become quasi-professionals, and that professionalization of journalism has had effects both positive (elevating ethical standards) and negative (institutionalizing illusory claims to neutrality). Too often journalists in the second half of the 20th century acted as part of the power structure rather than critics of it, as reporters and editors increasingly identified with the powerful people and institutions they were covering rather than being true adversaries.

In the 21st century, the idea of professional journalism – whatever its problems and limitations – is under assault from a pseudo-journalism driven by right-wing ideology. The assertion that the problem with media is that they are too liberal is attractive to many ordinary people who feel alienated from a centrist/liberal elite, which appears unconcerned with their plight. But the right-wing populism offered up by conservatives obscures the way in which elites from that perspective are equally unconcerned with the struggles of most citizens.

So, we sit at a strange time: Professional journalism is inadequate because of its ideological narrowness and subordination to power, but the attacks on professional journalism typically are ideologically even narrower and are rooted in a misguided analysis of power. Some of us are tempted to applaud the erosion of the model of professional journalism we find inadequate for democracy, but a more politicized model for journalism likely will follow the right-wing propaganda that has dominated in the United States in recent decades.

Does history offer insights as we struggle to create a more democratic news media? My reading of the past century leaves me focused on two points.

First, we have to be clear about what we mean by "democracy." The elites in the United States prefer a managerial conception of democracy based on the idea that in a complex society, ordinary people can participate most effectively by choosing between competing groups of political managers. A participatory conception understands democracy as a system in which ordinary people have meaningful ways to participate in the formation of public policy, not just in the selection of elites to rule them.

Second, we must recognize that expansions of individual freedom do not automatically translate into a deepening of democracy. Though legal guarantees of freedom of expression and political association are more developed today, there is less vibrant grassroots political organizing compared with the United States of the late 19th and early 20th centuries. In other writing I have referred to this as the "more freedom/ less democracy" paradox,[2] and it is central to understanding the perilous political situation we face.

The lesson I take away: Real democracy means real participation, which comes not from voting in elections or posting on blogs, but from a lifelong commitment to challenging power from the bottom up.

The problem, in short, is not just a media that doesn't serve democracy, but a political, economic, and social system that doesn't serve democracy. Paradoxically, radical movements have over the past century won an expansion of freedom, but much of the citizenry has become less progressive and less politically active at the grassroots. Concentrated wealth has adapted, becoming more sophisticated in its use of propaganda and skillful in its manipulation of the political process.

Journalism's claim to a special role in democracy is based on an assertion of independence. The corporate/commercial model puts limits on journalists' ability to follow crucial stories and critique systems and structures of power. Flinging the doors open to a more ideological journalism in a society dominated by well-funded right-wing forces will not create the space for truly independent journalism that challenges power.

The simple truth is that a more democratic media requires a more democratic culture and economy. The media critics in this volume articulated that idea in the context of their time. We need to continue that tradition.

---

2   Robert Jensen, *Citizens of the Empire: The Struggle to Claim Our Humanity* (San Francisco: City Lights Books, 2004), Chapter 4, "More Freedom, Less Democracy: American Political Culture in the Twentieth Century," pp. 55–76.

Acknowledgments

In 1995, we met as doctoral students at the University of Texas at Austin. At the time, we shared common interests in media law and ethics; professional backgrounds in journalism; and, the desire to work with Professor Robert Jensen, who ended up chairing both of our dissertation committees. Since we left UT in 1998, we have pursued varied research endeavors and have lived and worked at different universities. While geographically separated, we have always remained close because of our friendship, and our common interest in understanding and appreciating the disenfranchised, the underrepresented, the dissenters, and the minority voices. Our great affection toward and respect for our dissertation chair has also guided our paths, and continues to have immeasurable impact on our academic careers. This project would not exist without Bob Jensen's efforts to connect us to Rory Litwin. Rory's interest in publishing a book about press critiques during the Progressive Era led him to Jensen. Jensen led Rory to us. We are grateful to Bob Jensen for his continued support and guidance, and we are thankful that Rory has trusted us with this project.

We would also like to acknowledge and thank our colleagues at Louisiana State University's Manship School of Mass Communication, the Indiana University School of Journalism, and the Department of Mass Communications at Southern Illinois University Edwardsville, who have offered their encouragement and support of our efforts. We thank Manship School of Mass Communication graduate assistants Mallory Broussard and Kathryn Royals for helping us to edit and proofread the final manuscript. Finally, we want to acknowledge our families and thank them for their patience with this process.

Chapter One

Introduction
Press Criticism and the Progressive Era

At its core, this book is about highlighting press criticisms during the Progressive Era (1890–1920) that aimed to enhance the role of the press in a democracy, limit corporatization, and better utilize the press' capacity as an agent for social change. The critics reprinted here are mostly members of the press themselves, a phenomenon that is not necessarily uncharacteristic of U.S. press critiques leading up to this time.

Historians note that one of the first recognized articles critical of the U.S. press was printed in the *American Quarterly Review* in 1836, authored by British politicians and writers. But, after the Civil War, the lion's share of press criticism appeared in magazines and books, typically authored by journalists themselves. [3]

Historian Marion Tuttle Marzolf's book, *Civilizing Voices*, details the history of press criticism from 1880–1950, and suggests that the press paid close attention to the vigorous criticisms lobbied against it. While the press often made changes that addressed the concerns of the critics, Marzolf notes that there's no way of knowing how many of those changes can be directly traced back to specific critiques. She writes that press behavior typically changed over time, when press owners perceived public support for the criticism, thereby threatening a newspaper's audience and requiring change. When the criticisms were self-interested or deviated from mainstream values, Marzolf writes that they had little influence. [4]

Marzolf calls the form of journalism that existed during the Progres-

---

3   Hazel Dicken-Garcia, *Journalistic Standards in Nineteenth-Century America* (Madison: University of Wisconsin Press, 1989).
4   Marion Tuttle Marzolf, *Civilizing Voices* (New York: Longman, 1991).

sive Era "new journalism," because it was not rooted in partisan politics as was the case for much of the 19th century; and, because the press had already accepted a commercial model of news as commodity. She writes,

> The challenge this new style presented to society and to a budding profession offered an excellent opportunity for an examination of modern journalistic values and ideals. There was intense criticism of the press from outside and from inside. As the old and new values clashed, press critics kept raising the issues of moral purpose and democratic idealism to counter the strong forces of commercialization and impersonality. In this way, press criticism served as a civilizing force, a balancing agent, sometimes restraining and sometimes encouraging social change while protecting essential values.[5]

The essential journalistic values that most sought to protect centered on the role of a free press in a democracy – ideals of free speech and press, citizen involvement in self-government, and the press' responsibility to society.

This book republishes and historicizes some important voices and ideas about the power and the privilege of the press from the early 20th century. Within most chapters are articles and editorials by writers that many people today don't know – for example, Charles Edward Russell, Moorfield Storey, and Oswald Garrison Villard. The chapters that don't contain republished articles include biographical sketches and contextual information about these important people and about significant trends and events during this time that helped shape the press we know today. What is striking about their words and ideas is how relevant they still are in the 21st century.

The Progressive Era – Early Years

To understand the critiques and ideas expressed in subsequent chapters, it's useful to offer a brief overview of the Progressive Era. This era

---

5   Marzolf, p. 3.

is one of the most researched and discussed in American history. In many ways, a simple overview cannot do justice to the myriad of events and transitions that occurred in the U.S. during this important time. But, offering some general background is still helpful to understand the context in which journalists wrote about and challenged press practices during this era.

Chronologically, the time period commonly referred to as the Progressive Era in U.S. history spans from 1890 to 1920.[6] It was a period of meaningful political, social and economic change that would shape the United States and its domestic agenda for the remainder of the 20th century. Generally speaking, "progressivism" is the word used to describe a variety of responses to the economic and social problems that arose as a result of the rapid industrialization that took place in the decades after the Civil War. Progressivism started as a social movement, but it eventually transformed into a political movement. Its primary unifying principle was the belief that the government could play a positive role in solving social and economic problems through reform and regulation.

To underscore the significant changes that took place in this 30-year span, historian Lewis Gould observes that the major issues on the agenda of Congress in 1889–90 included the nature of currency, the use of tariffs to protect U.S. industry from foreign competition, and the fairness of elections in the South, where racial discrimination was still rampant. Big questions about how to grow and expand the U.S. economy drove public discourse, and the focus was on what role the government might play. Gould contrasts those discussions with what had happened by 1914. By 1914, the federal government had adopted policies that allowed it to regulate corporate and individual behavior, created a central banking mechanism (the Federal Reserve system), adopted the national income tax, established the Federal Trade Commission, and amended the Constitution so that the people – not the state legislatures – elected Senators to the U.S. Congress. "The shift from government as an instrument of promotion to a means of regulation was one of the key developments of

---

6   Most historians extend the period through 1920, but some choose to end the Progressive Era in 1914 at the start of World War I in Europe.

the progressive spirit."[7]

Although the reform campaigns that defined the Progressive Era began to appear in 1890, historians note that the origins of the era reach back to 1880, when people started to identify major social problems that some believed could be minimized with regulation or involvement by the government. The countervailing argument to the developing progressive sentiments was Social Darwinism. This way of thinking emphasized the "survival of the fittest"[8] idea applied in a social context – an extension of Darwin's theory of biological evolution and natural selection. Social Darwinists opposed governmental intervention because they regarded it as detrimental to "natural progress," particularly in relationship to the economy, but also with regard to the struggles between races. At this point in the 19th century, laissez-faire was the accepted economic doctrine, meaning that most business and economic transactions occurred with very little, if any, governmental intervention. Social Darwinists believed in laissez-faire, and supported what is often today called free market capitalism.[9]

But, by the 1890s, as the progressive spirit began to take hold, the U.S. began to consider alternatives to laissez-faire and to challenge the beliefs held by Social Darwinists. In 1888, a landslide Republican victory placed control of the House and Senate in the hands of the party, as well as saw Benjamin Harrison elected president. By 1890, the Republicans successfully expanded currency through the Sherman Silver Purchase Act, and passed the Sherman Antitrust Act as a way for government to regulate large corporations.

Despite these progressive-minded changes, the Republican's political dominance was short lived. Democrat Grover Cleveland became president in 1893, and he governed over one of the worst economic depressions in

---

7   Lewis L. Gould, *America in the Progressive Era, 1890–1914* (Harlow, England: Pearson Education, 2001), p. x.
8   British sociologist Herbert Spencer coined this well-known phrase in the 19th century.
9   John Whiteclay Chambers II, *The Tyranny of Change: America in the Progressive Era, 1890–1920* (New Brunswick, N.J.: Rutgers University Press, 2000), p. 5.

U.S. history. The depression was triggered by the failure of some British banks, and lasted four years. At the end of 1893, nearly a quarter of the American workforce was unemployed, and hundreds of businesses had failed. Workers went on strike, and labor unrest and violence spread across the country.[10] "Industrial violence, crime, disease and extensive urban poverty challenged American ideals of freedom, democracy, and a relatively classless and harmonious society" as a result of the depression.[11]

The U.S. also saw fairly explosive population growth during this time. By 1895, the U.S. population numbered 63 million, and most people still lived in rural areas. But, city growth had expanded since the end of the Civil War in 1865, and more than 22 million people now lived in towns or cities with populations greater than 2,500. In addition, this was a time of increased immigration to U.S. cities, with immigrants coming most frequently from southern and eastern Europe. Many of the immigrants were Catholic and Jewish, and the nativists – people who wanted to keep their cities homogenous and predominantly Anglo-Saxon Protestant – stirred tensions among differing groups of people.[12]

During the 1890s and into the turn of the century, the gap between the rich and the poor continued to grow. The U.S. was already a major economic power in the world, and it had also become industrialized. Manufacturing was on the rise, and the railroads had emerged as the nation's first big business. [13] According to historians,

> Industrialization ... seemed to be dividing the country into hostile classes: the extremely wealthy and the very poor. The new industrialized rich – plutocrats, many people called them – obtained unprecedented wealth and lived in opulent splendor. In 1900 the steel magnate Andrew Carnegie, shuttling between his baronial mansion on New York's Fifth Avenue and his castle in Scotland, made a tax-free profit of $23 million. At the same time, factories, mines, and

---

10   Gould, pp. 6–8; Chambers, pp. 3–5.
11   Chambers, p. 4.
12   Gould, p. 3; Chambers, p. 3.
13   Gould, p. 3.

railroads employed millions of unskilled and semi-skilled workers. Steelworkers worked twelve-hour shifts, six days a week and earned an average of $450 a year. ... Women earned less than men: in garment district sweatshops in New York City, they were paid only $5 for a six-day workweek, averaging $260 a year.[14]

To address some of the problems of poverty that were evidenced in the cities, some men and women opened "settlement houses," most famously in Chicago, New York, Boston and Philadelphia. These houses allowed philanthropic people to live among the poor and assist them with education, social activities, and by lending a helping hand. Some historians have suggested that the settlement house experience helped to create a generation of wealthy reformers who would subsequently fight for labor-related issues such as limiting the number of hours people worked, and inspecting factories and other workplaces for hazards and unsafe conditions. They also encouraged the regulation of public utilities.[15]

In addition to the labor and economic problems and severe poverty, the last decade of the 19th century was also filled with racial unrest and conflict that led to segregation. In the South in the period leading up to the 1890s, violence against African Americans was pervasive. Between 1882 and 1889, more than 2,500 black men and women were lynched. Election fraud, poll taxes, literacy laws, and violence prohibited many African Americans from voting in the South, and precluded their ability to run for elected office. During this time, nine out of ten African Americans lived in the region, and they made up about 40 percent of the total population of the South. [16]

By the 1890s, white leaders in the South had put into place segregation policies. The U.S. Supreme Court upheld the practice in 1896, deciding in *Plessy v. Ferguson* that segregation did not violate the 13th and 14th Amendments (the abolishment of slavery and the right to citizenship, due process and equal protection, respectively). This led to the notion of

---

14   Chambers, pp. 2–3.
15   Gould, p. 7.
16   Chambers, p. 9.

"separate but equal," that legally remained in place for more than half a century.[17]

Racial discrimination during this time was not limited to African Americans. Native Americans, Hispanics, Asians and others suffered from "pseudoscientific racism, a doctrine that held that there were inherent differences among human racial ethnic groups that determined cultural or individual achievement." Historian John Chambers adds, "the dominant national view in America at the turn of the century was that all other peoples were inferior to the white race and indeed to persons of western European descent."[18]

According to Gould, who has studied the Progressive Era for decades, "historians have long puzzled about why the United States did not erupt in social violence or more radical political change during the economic upheavals of the 1890s. To some extent there was a high degree of unrest ... yet, despite all the misery that attended the economic problems of the first half of the 1890s, citizens still retained a faith that the system could be changed by peaceful means. ... That faith would animate the progressive spirit," to close out the century.[19]

The Turn of the Century

By 1896, the economic depression lifted and the U.S. saw a return to prosperity, although the gap between the very rich and the very poor remained. The country saw a rise in the trusts and holding companies, and that would lead to a strong public confidence in the economic future of the country. The most critical economic development after the depression was the explosive growth of big business. In the seven years after 1897, more than 4,200 companies in the U.S. had become 257 corporations.[20]

A new topic for national discussion also had emerged – America's

---

17   *Plessy v. Ferguson*, 43 U.S. 537 (1896).
18   Chambers, p. 9. For a detailed look at how Americans of diverse backgrounds lived in this era, see Steven J. Diner, *A Very Different Age: Americans of the Progressive Era* (New York: Hill and Wang, 1998).
19   Gould, p. 17.
20   Gould, p. 25.

place as a world power – as the country entered the Spanish American War
in 1898. For more than three years, Cuba had staged a bloody revolution
against Spanish rule. Early in 1898, the U.S. attempted to negotiate a
settlement between the two. As that process deteriorated, the battleship
U.S.S. Maine was attacked in Havana harbor and more than 270 U.S.
military men died. The U.S. blamed Spain for the attack, despite a lack of
hard evidence. Public outrage at the attack and a Congress that wanted
war helped pushed President William McKinley to decide to intervene.
The U.S. entered the war in April 1898, and fought Spain in both Cuba
and in the Philippine Islands, which was also fighting for independence
from Spain at the time. At the end of the three-month war, which the
U.S. won handily, much debate ensued about the fate of the Philippine
Islands and American imperialism.[21]

In the end, the U.S. bought the Philippine Islands from Spain for $20
million dollars in The Treaty of Paris, and in short order the Philippine
American War started because the island nation wanted independence.
That war officially ended in 1902, but the U.S. continued to fight with
natives long after their defeat.[22] It was opposition to both the Spanish
American War and the Philippine American War that led to the creation of
the Anti-Imperialist League in 1898. Those who opposed the U.S. entering
the conflicts believed that such action threatened the strength of America's
democracy and ran against the traditional values of the country. They
pointed to the idea of an American empire running against the country's
basic ideals of self-governance and isolation. Anti-imperialists argued that
imperialism violated the basic idea of republicanism on which the country
was founded – namely, the need for the consent of the governed. They
also believed that fighting against European rivals could make war with
them a more likely prospect in the future. The anti-imperialists did not
root their objections in humanitarian, religious or economic arguments.[23]

---

21   Gould, p. 23.
22   The Philippines finally won autonomy in 1916, and the U.S. promised the
country eventual self-governance. That, though, did not occur until 1934. After World War II, in 1946, the Philippines were finally granted independence.
23   Gould, pp. 22–23.

People who supported the expansion of American influence in the world argued that the only way for the U.S. to become a world power was to meet competition from the existing world powers – Germany, France and Great Britain. If the U.S. failed to compete internationally, the imperialists argued, "it would become a second-rate power subject to the whims of stronger countries. There was also a significant component of racial superiority in American imperialism. ... As long as conquest was easy and the obligations of imperialism slight, many citizens found the adventure of empire an appealing experience."[24]

Noted anti-imperialists of the time included Mark Twain, Andrew Carnegie, former President Grover Cleveland, philosopher John Dewey, lawyer Moorfield Storey and journalist Oswald Garrison Villard. Noted proponents of imperialism were influential Senators Henry Cabot Lodge (Massachusetts) and Albert Beveridge (Indiana), and Rough Rider Theodore Roosevelt, who would become president in 1901.

The war in the Philippines and American imperialism became a major issue in the election of 1900. The Democratic candidate, William Jennings Bryan, made his anti-imperialist arguments central to his campaign. The Republican McKinley/Roosevelt ticket stood on the gains of the war in the Philippines and played down imperialism as a position, even though they supported it. Generally speaking, public opinion at the time suggested that Americans wanted to finish the war in the Philippines, but did not want to take on further expansion of the American empire. McKinley won re-election in a decisive victory, but the anti-imperialists had succeeded in convincing a majority of citizens that drawing back from policies of U.S. expansion in the world was a sensible notion. "Their criticisms also fostered a rethinking of American ideals as the century ended," and "made it possible for others to urge that national institutions be reexamined and reformed."[25]

Political scientist Eldon Eisenach notes the importance of winning over public opinion during the 1900 election, suggesting that progressive reformers at the turn of the century knew that their ultimate success

---

24   Gould, p. 23.
25   Gould, p. 25.

depended on gaining popular acceptance of their messages. Because progressives were powerful figures at prominent religious institutions, colleges and universities, in women's organizations and within news organizations, they had little trouble shaping the public agenda and defining the terms of the debate about a variety of progressive issues. But, they still faced two major barriers at this time. One was the presumption that public opinion equaled majority opinion, and that in turn, majority opinion meant "the preponderance of individual preferences."[26] The second barrier was that for there to be acceptance of whether or not public opinion equaled majority opinion as previously defined, the institutional test was assumed to be either the electoral system or the market, both of which were driven by individual preference.[27]

Eisenach writes, "the first task of the Progressives was to redefine the meaning of public and public opinion and to give opinion the legitimate power to act outside of the two arenas [market and electoral] that so overwhelmingly privileged local, isolated, and individual choices. In this process, the concept of public opinion could be transformed from an authoritative register of prevailing individual preferences into an engine of social control and transformation. In short, public opinion could become the authoritative will of a democratic nation."[28]

President Theodore Roosevelt

Roosevelt became president in 1901, after the assassination of President McKinley at the hands of an anarchist. Some historians have called Roosevelt one of the two most important national figures in the Progressive Era. Although impossible to know, Gould suggests that "something like" the progressive movement would still have emerged if McKinley had lived, but he argues that it likely would have been much less vigorous.[29]

---

26   Eldon J. Eisenach, *The Lost Promise of Progressivism* (Lawrence, Kan.: University Press of Kansas, 1994), p. 74.
27   Ibid.
28   Ibid.
29   Gould, p. 30. Gould suggests President Woodrow Wilson is the other.

Roosevelt was a popular president – he was considered a man of the people, even though he grew up in a wealthy New York City family, graduated from Harvard, and entered politics at an early age. When he became president, he created what is known as the "stewardship theory" of the office – "the president ... was the steward of the American people, and as the chief executive, should try to do the things that his fellow citizens wanted accomplished. If the Constitution did not expressly prohibit the president from doing some course of action, then [the president] ... had a duty to use his power for the benefit of the people."[30]

In 1902, Roosevelt told the Justice Department to file an antitrust suit against the newly formed Northern Securities Company. The company was a powerful railroad trust that was created by the owners of the vast majority of the railroad lines in the country, including J.P. Morgan, the steel and banking magnate. Presidents Cleveland and McKinley had not used the Sherman Antitrust Act as a way to break up the emerging powerful big businesses, perhaps because a Supreme Court decision in 1895 significantly limited the scope and power of the law.[31] Roosevelt wanted to challenge the court's 1895 ruling and revitalize the Sherman Act. The government won a narrow decision in its case when the Supreme Court ruled in its favor in 1904, and the Northern Securities Company was dissolved.[32]

Roosevelt's challenge to the railroad trust and to subsequent others earned him a reputation as a trust-buster, even though he wasn't, in reality, an opponent of big business.[33] Rather, Roosevelt made distinc-

---

30   Gould, p. 32.
31   *U.S. v. E.C. Knight*, 156 U.S. 1 (1895).
32   *Northern Securities Co. v. United States*, 193 U.S. 197 (1904). For a thorough discussion of this case and Roosevelt's relationship with the Supreme Court during this time, see John E. Semonche, *Charting the Future: The Supreme Court Responds to a Changing Society, 1890–1920* (Westport, Conn.: Greenwood Press, 1978), pp. 165–200.
33   In the seven years that followed the Northern Securities ruling, 44 other antitrust cases resulted in monopoly breakups, although most of these occurred under President William Howard Taft. Taft used the Sherman Antitrust Act to break up all monopolies, while Roosevelt saw the application of the law appropriate only in cases of clear corporate misbehavior. See Gould, p. 57.

tions between good and bad trusts, with the good ones having some social usefulness. He maintained that the government not only had a right to control the trusts, but that it also had a duty in instances of bad trusts (those that were predatory or had no social usefulness) to take action.[34]

While Roosevelt's presidency was now beginning to allow a progressive agenda to take shape, one area was noticeably absent – efforts to create a more equitable society for African Americans. In the early years of the 20th century, racial segregation was now an accepted fact of life. Lynching remained common in the South, and there were no longer any black members of Congress because the majority of blacks were barred from the political process in the South. For most whites, whether progressive or conservative, the status of African Americans in the U.S. was not on the agenda for reform throughout most of the Progressive Era.

Roosevelt was reelected to the presidency in 1904 by a landslide. Historians note that the years between 1905 and 1917 represent the peak of progressivism nationally, largely because Roosevelt's reelection opened the door.[35] This is also the peak of the power of the muckrakers, journalists who played a significant role in advancing the progressive movement even in the earliest part of the Progressive Era.

The Muckrakers

Roosevelt is credited with coining the term "muckraker" in a 1906 speech in which he was making reference to a character in John Bunyan's *Pilgrim's Pride*: "... you may recall the description of the Man with the Muck-rake, the man who could look no way but downward with the muck-rake in his hands." Roosevelt cautioned people not to stay focused on the filth or "the muck," but noted that the social, economic and political evils of the time required "relentless exposure and attack" by the press. "I hail as a benefactor every writer or speaker, every man who, on the platform, or in book, magazine, or newspaper, with merciless severity makes such

---

34   Gould, pp. 32–34; see also George E. Mowry, *Theodore Roosevelt and the Progressive Movement* (Madison: University of Wisconsin Press, 1946).
35   Chambers, p. 283.

attack, provided always that he in his turn remembers that the attack is of use only if it is absolutely truthful."[36]

The term muckraking today generally refers to a group of journalists who were crusading against the varying problems with which the country wrestled during the Progressive Era, beginning in the 1890s, although most famously after the turn of the century. Historian Louis Filler perhaps captures the character of the muckrakers and their publications best:

> There appeared in certain magazines a new, moral, radical type of writing ... These writers savagely exposed grafting politicians, criminal police, tenement eyesores. They openly attacked the Church. They defended labor in disputes which in no way concerned them personally, decried child exploitation, wrote pro-suffragist articles, and described great businesses as soulless and anti-social. These writers, using the most sordid details to make their points, shocked and bewildered the conservative reader. ... To the common people, however, the new writing was as gripping as it was educational: they had never known that business and politics could be so interesting. Responding to their rising interest, a dozen magazines were soon competing for popular attention with newer and more vivid exposés, in which they named names and used photographs in order to establish the truth of their claims. Popular magazines had been born twenty years before; now, with this new means of stimulating circulation, they multiplied and grew mature overnight, and infected even the staid periodicals with their new theme.[37]

---

36   Donald P. DeNevi, Helen M. Friend, and John Bookout, *Muckrakers and Robber Barons: The Classic Era, 1902–1912* (Danville, Calif.: Replica Books, 1973), pp. 3–4. See also, Wayne Andrews (Ed.), *The Autobiography of Theodore Roosevelt, Condensed from the Original Edition, Supplemented by Letters, Speeches, and Other Writings* (New York: Scribner's, 1958), pp. 246–47. Despite Roosevelt's words seeming to encourage more muckraking, at the time of this speech he was irritated with some muckraking journalists who were, in his view, spending too much time investigating big business and were pushing too hard for radical reforms that went too far. See Gould, p. 45.

37   Louis Filler, *The Muckrakers* (University Park, Pa.: The Pennsylvania State University Press, 1976), pp. 9–10.

Most muckraking was journalistic in style – it involved extensive investigation and reporting, but was written in a way easily accessible to a wide audience. Most muckraking articles appeared in magazines, but some of the muckrakers' work was also published as newspaper columns, editorials and as books. Many historians have argued that some newspaper reporters, like Jacob Riis, deserve attention as early muckrakers and crusading journalists.[38]

Riis was a police reporter for the *New York Tribune* and the *New York Sun* between 1877 and 1899. He reported frequently about the tenement districts in New York, declaring his own "personal war" on the "exploiting employers and landlords" who were so largely responsible for the horrible conditions in which so many men, women and children lived. Riis' reporting was so effective, hundreds of readers joined his efforts to try to rid the city of its awful slums by providing money and influence. His books, *How the Other Half Lives* (1890) and *The Children of the Poor* (1892) are two examples of pioneering muckraking works that pre-date what many consider muckraking's golden age of about 1903–1912.[39]

Earlier in this chapter, the explosive growth of the U.S. population between the end of the Civil War and the turn of the century was noted; daily newspapers in the U.S. also saw unparalleled growth at this time. By 1899, more than 1,600 daily newspapers were published in the U.S.[40] Industrialization and a move toward the mass production of goods meant that industry needed avenues for national distribution and advertising. Department stores and newspapers were clear vehicles for these two tasks, respectively.

Newspapers soon became big businesses themselves, still offering local news and editorials, but adapting to a new style that also gave readers access to national news and trends, syndicated columns and features. This "new journalism" drew new readers because of an increasingly educated

---

38   John M. Harrison and Harry H. Stein, *Muckraking: Past, Present and Future* (University Park, Pa.: The Pennsylvania State University Press, 1973), p. 4.
39   Ibid, p. 3.
40   Gould, p. 28.

and literate population, and because of the new style of writing, that brought new enthusiasm and energy to the newspaper.[41]

Joseph Pulitzer, for whom Jacob Riis and many other famous crusading journalists would work, saw New York City during the 1880s as the perfect place to develop "new journalism" that also fit his desire to "create a truly democratic paper that served not only the masses, but humanitarian causes."[42] His *New York World* soon was publishing exposés about bribery and corruption in city government, and put forth campaigns to help the poor, while at the same time offering readers comic strips, puzzles and short stories.

The "old" journalists of the time – those still attached to partisan agendas and literary, longer form styles of essay writing – responded by creating new magazines that maintained their literary style, and focused on addressing important social and political issues of the day. Some of the magazines featured debates on the role of journalism, given the division between the new and old styles of providing news. While the new journalism was often sensationalistic and focused on building circulation (most notably in New York City), it still had a strong desire to improve social conditions. The two most famous New York newspapers at the turn of the century – Pulitzer's *New York World* and William Randolph Hearst's *New York Journal* – were both sympathetic to labor and immigrants, and published exposés that went well beyond the normal scope of daily journalism.[43]

Historians note that muckraking is traditionally associated with three major press traditions in the U.S. – investigative journalism, advocacy journalism, and sensationalistic journalism, sometimes also called "yellow journalism." Not all sensationalistic journalism was yellow, but all yellow journalism was sensational. Yellow journalism was known for manufacturing the news, writing misleading headlines and offering lurid details about taboo subjects. Yet, much sensational and yellow journalism

---

41   Marzolf, p. 8; See also Edwin Emery and Michael Emery, *The Press and America*, 5th ed. (Englewood Cliffs, N.J.: Prentice-Hall, 1984), pp. 253–280.
42   Marzolf, p. 9.
43   Ibid.

during the 1890s supported political and social crusades in largely the same way the muckrakers did. Although Pulitzer's *New York World* and Hearst's *New York Journal* are both famously associated with sensational journalism and its extension into yellow journalism, both employed some important muckraking and crusading journalists like Riis and Charles Edward Russell (who were not yellow journalists, but who did sensationalize their writing).[44]

While debate exists about how much muckraking really occurred in the sensational, yellow journalism that pervaded the 1890s, no historians question the importance of *McClure's Magazine* to the muckraking movement. *McClure's* is associated mostly with the investigative and advocacy journalism traditions, both of which "expose or reveal fresh facts or patterns of meaning to their audiences and sometimes offer solutions to depicted problems. ... [M]uckraking work, already selective in facts and emphasis to elicit indignation or anger, proceeds beyond the investigative form to indicate how extensive, not unique, are the practices and ideas exposed."[45]

McClure's is perhaps the most celebrated muckraking publication, partially because it helped to create some of the most famous muckraking writers of the early 20th century. Because of his awareness of the public's concern about the large and powerful trusts, and corruption within politics and municipal government, publisher Samuel S. McClure directed two of his reporters to explore how the trusts worked and how municipal politics operated.

He asked Ida Tarbell to investigate John D. Rockerfeller's Standard Oil Company; he asked Lincoln Steffens to explore municipal corruption in major cities such as Minneapolis and St. Louis. *McClure's* January 1903 issue hit the newsstands with three powerful exposés. Tarbell's second installment that documented the history of the Standard Oil Company appeared, along with Steffens' "The Shame of Minneapolis," and Ray Stannard Baker's "The Right to Work," which reported on the working conditions in the nation's coalmines. In this issue, McClure also included

---

44   Harrison and Stein, p. 16.
45   Ibid, p. 14.

an editorial that drew attention to the three investigative pieces, and he noted that while the three subjects appeared to be different, they actually all addressed "the threat to democracy from good people doing nothing. It became a constant theme of the muckrakers."[46]

McClure's model – he wanted stories that would "shock readers into demanding social reforms," based on the reporting of fact, naming names, personifying social conflict and writing absorbing narratives – was immediately replicated. *Cosmopolitan, Collier's, Everybody's, Arena, Pearson's, Hampton's, Ladies Home Journal* and many general circulation magazines soon put exposé, muckraking stories on their covers. Between 1903 and 1912, historians estimate that more than 2,000 investigative articles appeared in American magazines. Most made the case for widespread social and political reforms that mirrored the causes embraced by progressives. The muckrakers were offering their readers an education, and they were working to "distinguish, examine, and judge whatever ... seemed to improve or lessen humankind and society. The thrust for moral social improvement [was] part of their design."[47]

The Progressive Era, 1904–1920

After Roosevelt's reelection in 1904, "the spirit of progressive reform became a dominant element in American public life."[48] The economic prosperity of the nation was stable, and people were generally optimistic about the future of the country. Still, the nation wrestled with the serious problems of child labor, racial unrest, and corruption in politics. People had grown weary of partisan politics, and wanted a new form of campaigning that relied more heavily on discussion of issues and appeals to reason, not to emotions and partisanship. As a result, campaigns dur-

---

46   James Aucion, *The Evolution of American Investigative Journalism* (Columbia: University of Missouri Press, 2005), p. 32. That January 1903 edition of *McClure's* quickly sold out its 400,000 copies.
47   David Mark Chalmers, *The Social and Political Ideas of the Muckrakers* (New York: The Citadel Press, 1964), p. 15; Harrison and Stein, p. 16; Aucion, p. 33.
48   Gould, p. 38.

ing this period became more advertising oriented and cost more money. Rising costs meant greater dependence on corporate contributions for political campaigns.[49]

The impact of muckraking journalism was also now felt more directly than it had been. For example, Upton Sinclair's book *The Jungle,* which detailed the sickening conditions of the meatpacking industry in Chicago, led to legislation calling for federal inspections of meatpacking plants. The outrage over Sinclair's writings about the meatpacking industry also led to the emergence of the Pure Food and Drug Act in 1906. The intensity with which some muckraking journalists were scrutinizing some Senators and their connections to big business led Roosevelt to comment on the practice of muckraking in his previously noted 1906 speech. He also cautioned journalists not to go too far in their criticisms.[50]

Partially in response to the labor issues in the country, the 1906 election cycle saw an increase in influence of the growing Socialist Party. This created a division within the progressive movement. The Socialists didn't believe in capitalism and encouraged much stronger governmental reforms. Roosevelt and other progressives saw socialism as too radical. They believed that the socialists' assault on capitalism and private property went too far. Instead, they supported the judicious use of governmental power to make useful changes. The addition of the Socialist Party as a meaningful player on the political scene resulted in the Republicans and Democrats both reevaluating where they stood on issues of regulation and government control. While the 1906 election didn't resolve the emerging tensions about government regulation in either the Republican or Democratic Party, it did see them each move closer to the positions they hold today.[51]

In 1908, the political tensions remained. Voters elected the man that Roosevelt had a strong hand in helping become the Republican nominee for president, William Howard Taft. Taft was Roosevelt's Secretary of War, and someone who was moving away from the progressive positions

---

49   Gould, p. 41.
50   Gould, pp. 43–46.
51   Gould, pp. 46–47.

that many in the Republican Party still held. Many of the strong progressives that favored more government regulation and stronger limitations on capitalism left the Republican Party for the Socialist Party. Some stayed, and they created their own "progressive faction" within the party, led by Wisconsin Senator Robert LaFollette. Democrats had hoped that the split within the Republican Party would lead them to victory; but, Roosevelt's personal leadership of the Taft campaign and the party's resources and experience resulted in a Taft victory.[52]

During Taft's term in office and the election of Democrat Woodrow Wilson in 1912, the U.S. experienced a period of political upheaval. The Socialist Party had reached the height of its influence, and the Republicans further divided into warring factions. By 1914, the Republican Party was split between progressive and conservative factions. A variety of interest groups that had emerged during this time made meaningful gains as the powerful party system was shaken. The women's suffrage movement gained momentum, as did efforts toward the prohibition of alcohol, restrictions on immigration, outlawing child labor, creating a federal income tax and calling for the direct election of senators.[53]

Prior to Wilson's election, Roosevelt had been critical of President Taft, whom he believed did not share his vision of progressivism. In 1910, after returning from a year in Africa, Roosevelt embarked on a speaking tour across the U.S. that highlighted his views on the issues of the day. He did this, historians suggest, to save the Republican Party from Taft and his policies. Called "New Nationalism," Roosevelt set out to articulate a new role for the government in dealing with social issues. He elaborated on his stewardship theory of the presidency, telling crowds that executive power was the steward of the public welfare and that the national government needed to take on a broader regulatory role.

> The New Nationalism ideology represented a significant elaboration of one vein of American progressivism. It embodied Roosevelt's faith in the strong presidency, his commitment to a broader program

---

52   Gould, p. 52.
53   Gould, pp. 53–54.

of regulation, and a growing conviction that the nation must address the plight of women, children, and the underprivileged generally. Roosevelt did not include in his concerns the status of minorities. But his articulation of themes of justice, equality, and more power for the state looked forward to the goals of liberalism as they would emerge in Franklin D. Roosevelt's New Deal and Lyndon Johnson's Great Society.[54]

Roosevelt and Taft continued to move farther away from each other as the 1912 presidential election approached. Gould calls the intraparty fight for the Republican presidential nomination "one of the legendary confrontations in the political history of the United States." After Roosevelt failed to secure the Republican nomination, he called his own convention and created the Progressive Party. The presidential election became a four-way race between Taft, Roosevelt, Eugene Debs, the Socialist Party candidate, and Wilson, the Democrat. Wilson knew he could not run as a conventional democrat because of Roosevelt's presence in the race. So, he worked with famous Boston lawyer Louis D. Brandeis to craft his own progressively oriented vision for the future.[55]

Wilson ran on a platform that came to be called the New Freedom. In essence, the New Freedom argued that it was competition among business that would ensure monopoly would not prevail, and that the real enemy to the interests of Americans was the bigness of businesses that created a concentration of economic power. Wilson argued that the government should use antitrust laws to break up these concentrations of economic power, but otherwise allow businesses to compete to protect against monopoly. Wilson had been looking for a way to oppose corporate power but also to not expand governmental regulation. During his campaign he denounced the impact of corporate influence – child labor, overcrowded cities, industrial accidents. He claimed that Roosevelt, because of his lack of opposition to big business, would work with big business to create

---

54   Gould, p. 58.
55   Gould, p. 65. Brandeis would go on to serve as a highly influential justice on the U.S. Supreme Court, appointed by Wilson in 1916.

regulations and administrative agencies. In effect, he suggested that Roosevelt's reform agencies would be pawns of the larger corporations. As Gould notes,

> The dispute between Roosevelt's New Nationalism and Wilson's New Freedom in 1912 posed a classic choice for progressives. In dealing with social problems, how much should an activist regulatory government try to accomplish? Roosevelt said that the nation must go further in the direction of government supervision. Wilson countered that there were ways to achieve Roosevelt's aims without broadening government power to the extent that the former president advocated. The enforcement of existing laws ... would be all that was necessary. The argument between these two candidates showed how far the nation had moved in the direction of progressive ideas by 1912. Programs for social justice that would have been deemed impossibly intrusive into private affairs in 1890 were now on the national agenda. The 1912 election set the terms of debate on domestic issues for decades to come.[56]

The outcome of the election was that the Democrats regained control of the presidency and of both houses of Congress. Roosevelt finished second in the election, followed by Taft and Debs. Debs managed to draw the largest Socialist vote to date, receiving 900,000 ballots in his favor (six percent of the vote). Socialism was considered a respectable political force in 1912, and its growing popularity showed that there was an audience for even more radical change in the country.

Nearly two years after Wilson's election, World War I broke out in Europe. Historians agree that this was a turning point for progressivism, and marks the start of its decline. The U.S. entered the war in 1917. By 1918, when the Republicans regained control of Congress "most of the basic spirit of progressive reform" had vanished. As president between 1913 and 1921, Wilson managed to make the Democrats "the party of governmental activism and regulation" to a degree that would have been unthinkable when Cleveland was president in 1893. "With two progres-

---

56   Gould, p. 66.

sive presidents in Roosevelt and Wilson, reform received a legitimacy that it would not have obtained if it had been associated with only one of the two major parties."[57]

Prophets of the Fourth Estate

Historians continue to assert that the Progressive Era is ripe for study, even though it is well documented. Where more work remains, some suggest, is in the exploration of how this period related to the time that came before and after it, and in how specific individuals and groups contributed to the progressive movement.[58] This book does both in the context of the press. The following explorations of how the press evolved during this period have terrific relevance to 21st century journalism. In addition, the reprinted critiques of the press have received little, if any, attention.

Chapter two explains the life of one of the most influential muckraking journalists of his time. Charles Edward Russell, a famous New York City reporter and editor, believed that newspapers should hold elected officials accountable. When he supervised the editorial pages of Joseph Pulitzer's *New York World* in the late 1890s, Russell "embraced the poor, mocked the blue-blooded wealthy, and crusaded especially against the emerging plutocratic monopolies that many felt were threatening democracy."[59] He left the *World* in 1897 for the highly sensational *New York Journal*, but found harmony with publisher William Randolph Hearst because both believed that citizens needed a voice to protect themselves from the growing power of corporate monopolies.

Russell began muckraking in the early 1900s, and most of his stories embraced the progressives' arguments of the time – that private capital was out of control, that wealthy industrial leaders were killing competition, and

---

57   Gould, p. 79.
58   David R. Colburn and George E. Pozzetta (Eds), *Reform and Reformers in the Progressive Era* (Westport, Conn.: Greenwood Press, 1983).
59   Robert Miraldi, *The Pen is Mightier: The Muckraking Life of Charles Edward Russell* (New York, Palgrave MacMillan, 2003), p. 81.

that the capitalistic system was largely to blame. In 1909, Russell began exposing what today we would call social justice issues. For example, he told his readers about the deplorable conditions in federal and state prisons, and wrote extensively about abuses of prisoner labor. Russell also cared about race issues, although instead of writing extensively on the subject he became directly involved. In 1909, Russell chaired the first National Negro Conference – a meeting that led to the formation of the National Association for the Advancement of Colored People (NAACP).

In 1908, Russell joined the Socialist Party, and by 1910 he ran as the party's candidate for Governor of New York. That would become one of four unsuccessful runs for public office. All of his campaigns focused on addressing unfair labor practices, equality, and eradicating poverty.

In 1916, Russell returned to journalism and became a war correspondent for the Newspaper Enterprise Association. This is the same year that he split with the Socialist Party over his views that World War I was necessary because he believed democracy around the world was threatened. The human atrocities and horrors he witnessed in war zones made him a staunch supporter of President Wilson, who invited him on a diplomatic mission to Russia.

Chapter three republishes an article that Russell wrote for *Pearson's Magazine* that offers readers insights into the day-to-day operations of a newspaper. Russell wrote this during the time he was running for public office, and authoring books and writing for the muckraking magazines on the side. The article is the first in a series written by Russell, and focuses on the impact of advertising on the news and on newspaper ownership. The series as a whole took on the problems of advertiser influence, newspaper ownership, media monopolies, efforts to shut down the muckraking magazines, and efforts by corporations to unduly influence public thought and opinion through the traveling lecture series' of the time.

Efforts to impact public opinion in the early 20th century are addressed in chapter four. Worth noting is the power of the public lecture circuits of the time. The primary criticism of the circuits was that they were ripe for both public and private pressures to control who spoke and on which topics, because the organizational structure relied on local committees and platform managers. Writer and educator Glenn Frank suggested in a 1919 *Century Magazine* article that the tent circuits should have followed a model like the Ford Hall Forum in Boston, which was founded in 1908, and still exists today as the nation's oldest continuously operating free public lecture series.[60] Frank wrote, "The Lyceum and Chautauqua represent an extensive national machinery of influence, reaching into all sorts of communities. With the exception of the church and the public school, no word-of-mouth institution equals its scope."[61]

Russell and many of his muckraking colleagues knew the Chautauqua circuit well from the inside. Russell, Ida Tarbell, Lincoln Steffens and Will Irwin all were paid to give lectures, and between 1910 and 1912 Russell was a regular performer. In his autobiography, Russell acknowledged that the Chautauquas were meant to blend culture and profit, but that he thought it was "a great educational factor" in raising public consciousness about many important issues.

Chapter five offers a detailed look at the evolution of advertising and how it impacted the content in newspapers. It also explores how postal regulation reforms affected the press. President Taft had taken on the challenge of postal reform and made no headway. Muckraking journalists argued that Taft was using postal reform to try to silence muckraking magazines critical of his administration. Historians believe this was a piece of Taft's agenda in pushing the reforms, and is part of the reason he failed. He was a president who did not have a good relationship with the press as a whole.[62]

---

60   Theodore Morrison, *Chautauqua: A Center for Education, Religion, and the Arts in America* (Chicago: The University of Chicago Press, 1974) p. 183. See also Kevin Mattson, *Creating a Democratic Public: The Struggle for Urban Participatory Democracy During the Progressive Era* (State College, Pa.: The Pennsylvania State University Press, 1998) p. 45; and, www.fordhallforum. org.
61   Glenn Frank, "The Parliament of the People," *Century Magazine*, July, 1919.
62   Richard B. Kielbowicz, "Origins of the Second-Class Mail Category and the Business of Policymaking, 1863–1879," *Journalism Monographs*, no. 96 (April 1986), pp. 469–471. See also George Juergens, *News from the White House: The Presidential-Press Relationship in the Progressive Era* (Chicago: University of Chicago Press, 1982), p. 118.

Chapter six offers a biographical sketch of Moorfield Storey, one of the founders of the NAACP and the Anti-Imperialist League. Storey channeled his anti-imperialist position into the role of defender of equal rights for humanity. His concern over the treatment of Filipinos during the Philippine American War seamlessly led to his work on behalf of the rights of black Americans, Native Americans and immigrants.

Storey was elected the first president of the NAACP, a position he would hold until his death. As president, Storey argued some of the Association's most contentious – and successful – cases. His skill as a lawyer well served the association in its early legal efforts to bring about racial equality at a time when lynching and the destruction of black homes were rampant in American cities. The early years of the NAACP, during which Storey served both as president and chief legal counsel, saw some of the NAACP's greatest legal successes.[63] Included in chapter six is one of Storey's writings about the state of the daily press in America after World War I.

Chapter seven highlights the significance of journalist Oswald Garrison Villard, as well as two important publications – the *Atlantic Monthly* and *The Nation*. Garrison, grandson of famous abolitionist William Lloyd Garrison and son of journalist and railroad magnate Henry Villard, had two prominent strains that ran strongly through his life – capitalist expansion and humanitarian reform. Although these two strains seem incompatible, they ultimately resulted in Villard becoming a prominent liberal, journalist and activist. The wealth with which he lived did not push him away from humanitarian causes. [64]

In 1912, Villard publicly supported Wilson for President of the United States. He believed that Wilson would advance "Negro rights" and would

---

63   Mark V. Tushnet, *The NAACP's Legal Strategy Against Segregated Education, 1925–1950* (Chapel Hill: The University of North Carolina Press, 1987). This book, while dealing mostly with the period after Storey's death, does include some of Storey's most influential legal efforts on behalf of the NAACP.
64   D. Joy Humes, *Oswald Garrison Villard, Liberal of the 1920's* (Syracuse, N.Y.: Syracuse University Press, 1960); Michael Wreszin, *Oswald Garrison Villard, Pacifist at War* (Bloomington, Ind.: Indiana University Press, 1965); Gilbert Murray, *Liberality and Civilization* (London: George Allen, Ltd., 1938), p. 31.

institute women's suffrage. But, after Wilson's election, Villard was disappointed that Wilson supported policies of segregation. He attracted
Wilson's ire when he used Wilson's own writings about democracy to
criticize the president. Villard noted that nowhere in Wilson's writings
"do we find any indication that his democracy is not strictly limited by
the sex line and the color line."[65]

In 1918, Villard devoted most of his time to *The Nation*. On February
1, 1918, Villard was owner, publisher and editor of *The Nation* and served
in this capacity until 1932. Villard's *Nation* saw record circulation – in
his first two years as editor, readership grew from 7,200 to more than
38,000. According to historian Dollena Joy Hume, *The Nation* and *The
New Republic* became influential voices of American liberalism between
1918 and 1932.

In addition to maintaining his interest in fighting for civil rights, Villard was also someone who scrutinized his own profession. He was a vocal
critic of newspapers he thought were unduly influenced by advertisers,
and he was concerned about the "disappearing daily" newspaper, which he
felt was vulnerable to the trend of news as a "great business enterprise."[66]

Chapter eight republishes some of Villard's writing from *The Nation*
and explores the dangers of press consolidation. It also examines trends
toward the censorship of a free press and of free speech during World War
I. Villard points out in one of his republished writings in this chapter that
many people who opposed the U.S. entering World War I were not able to
have their voices heard in the large daily newspapers. He wrote, "In this
situation many are turning to the Socialistic press as their one refuge."

It may not be surprising, then, that socialists were one of the primary
targets of new legislation aimed at stopping their perceived and potential
impact on society and on U.S. politics during the war. Because socialists and other "radicals" were clearly the target, and because the U.S.

---

65   Oswald Garrison Villard, *Fighting Years: Memoirs of a Liberal Editor*
(New York: Harcourt, Brace & Co., 1939), p. 240. See also Ray Stannard
Baker, *Woodrow Wilson: Life and Letters* (Garden City, N.Y.: Doubleday & Co.,
Inc., 1931), Vol. III, pp. 221–22.
66   Oswald Garrison Villard, *The Disappearing Daily, Some Chapters in
American Newspaper Evolution* (New York: Alfred Knopf, 1944), p. v.

had entered a period of extraordinary patriotism that led to a powerful marginalization of dissenting voices, much of the U.S. Congress did not object to the passage of new legislation that took aim at limiting activities that would aid the "enemy."

In June 1917, President Wilson signed the Espionage Act into law. It held that when the U.S. is at war, no one can willfully cause or attempt to cause insubordination in the military; that people could not willfully obstruct recruiting; that people could not willfully make or convey false reports or false statements with the intent to interfere with the operations or success of the military or navy or to promote the success of its enemies; and, that any printed material of any kind that is in violation of the Espionage Act provisions could not be mailed through the U.S. postal service.[67]

Historian Bob Mann notes that Congress removed a specific press censorship provision in the early versions of the law. He quotes Massachusetts Senator Henry Cabot Lodge from the May 11, 1917 *Congressional Record*, who said, "To attempt to deny to the press all legitimate criticism either of Congress or the Executive is going very dangerously far."[68] Lodge and other members of Congress believed they had removed all of the provisions from the law that would suppress free speech and press. But, they were mistaken.

In the few years after the passage of the Espionage Act, the Justice Department would prosecute 2,168 people under the law, convicting 1,055 for speaking against the war. Of those convicted, most were leaders of the socialist Industrial Workers of the World labor union (known as Wobblies) or leaders in the Socialist Party.[69]

Chapter nine examines how the intersection of public relations, propaganda and the general use of publicity by public agencies and businesses in the early 20th century led to the notion that public opinion could be

---

67   The Espionage Act of 1917, as cited in *Schenk v. United States*, 249 U.S. 47 (1919), 47.
68   Robert Mann, *Wartime Dissent in America: A History and Anthology* (New York: Palgrave Macmillan, 2010), p. 72.
69   Mann, p. 92; see also Harry N. Scheiber, *The Wilson Administration and Civil Liberties* (Ithaca, N.Y.: Cornell University Press, 1960), pp. 46–47.

influenced by the press and used to accomplish policy goals.[70] At points during the time period of World War I (1917–1918), it was difficult for citizens and journalists to determine what was useful information instead of propaganda. In "The Failure of the Fourth Estate," a reprinted article by Donald Wilhelm, he recognizes the danger to the public when press autonomy is compromised by concerted efforts to influence the news. While many people took note of governmental propagandistic efforts to influence public opinion during World War I, few seemed to recognize the influence of the public relations practitioners of the time who represented corporate interests.

All of the press criticisms during the Progressive Era that are highlighted in these pages envisioned a free press that would promote democracy, limit the corporatization and commodification of the news, and better utilize the press' capacity as an agent for social change. While much of this did occur during the Progressive Era, these criticisms show that enlightened men and women could see that the emerging profession of journalism was still falling far short. In these critiques are ideas that we still discuss today. Media critics of the 21st century hope that even if the commercialization of media is a foregone conclusion, that media still can find some ability to impact government and society for the betterment of humanity.

---

70   Timothy E. Cook, *Governing With the News: The News Media as a Political Institution* (Chicago: The University of Chicago Press, 1998), pp. 49–51.

Chapter 2

Charles Edward Russell

Although not well known today, Charles Edward Russell was one of the most influential muckraking journalists of the early 20th century. Born in Iowa in 1860, Russell grew up around political activism and newspapers. His father, Edward Russell, was the editor of the Davenport, Iowa, *Gazette* for more than three decades. Edward Russell was the founder of the Scott County, Iowa, Republican Party the same year Charles was born, and was a staunch supporter of Abraham Lincoln. For a short period of time he served as postmaster in Davenport – appointed by Lincoln in 1865, then removed from office by President Andrew Johnson, whom Russell outspokenly opposed. Edward Russell was an abolitionist before the Civil War, and afterward was someone who challenged the railroads and other large trusts for practices that harmed farmers and communities through a variety of unfair practices designed to maximize the wealth of the few. [71]

According to historian Robert Miraldi, Edward Russell valued his role as an editor because he considered the press to be "the guardian and nourisher of civic virtue." He told his son that the role of the press was to "terrify evil-doers and arouse the communal conscience." Charles Edward Russell shared many of his father's views, and developed a respect and admiration for journalism by working for his father in the summers. He enjoyed hearing stories of the big city newspapers from the "tramp printers," craftsmen who travelled around the country working for various newspapers, including Russell's *Davenport Gazette*. From an early

---

71 Book Reviews, "These Were my Forebears, *A Pioneer Editor in Early Iowa: A Sketch of the Life of Edward Russell*" (Washington, D.C.: Ransdell Inc., 1941), by his son Charles Edward Russell, *The Crisis*, September 1941, p. 300; see also, Alice Felt Tyler, *Freedom's Ferment: Phases of American Social History to 1860* (Minneapolis: University of Minnesota Press, 1944).

age, Charles Edward Russell dreamed of moving to New York to work as a reporter.[72]

Charles Edward Russell was also influenced by the speeches of noted abolitionist Wendell Phillips. After the Civil War, Phillips advocated for women's suffrage, equal rights for Native Americans, and the labor movement. During the two years he attended a college-prep school, St. Johnsbury Academy in Vermont, Russell was not only exposed to many of Phillips' famous speeches, but also to some early magazine exposés that challenged the new industrial power. [73]

In 1881, Russell read an article written by Henry Demarest Lloyd in the *Atlantic Monthly*, which exposed how John D. Rockefeller built his great oil monopoly, Standard Oil Corporation. Russell later read Lloyd's famous book *Wealth Against Commonwealth* (1894), which expanded on his denunciation of Rockefeller and Standard Oil, and attacked the notion of industrial monopolies. Russell himself later reflected that the Lloyd book had a tremendous impact on him: "[I was] swept by an increasing and irresistible interest. ... This industrial development of which [the U.S.] had been so proud was a source, not of strength, but of fatal weakness." Russell concluded that Rockefeller and others hadn't created a "great business enterprise," but instead what they had accomplished amounted to "no more than greed praying upon need."[74]

---

72   Robert Miraldi, *The Pen is Mightier: The Muckraking Life of Charles Edward Russell* (New York, Palgrave MacMillan, 2003), pp. 21–23. This chapter cites Miraldi often because very little has been written about Russell, even in books that detail the phenomenon of muckraking. The most famous muckrakers – Russell's contemporaries – all appear prominently in books and articles about this period in American journalism. These include Lincoln Steffens, Ida Tarbell, David Graham Phillips, Upton Sinclair, and Ray Stannard Baker. Miraldi believes the lack of attention historically paid to Russell may be because he had no one topic that made him famous, while all of the others had one primary issue attached to his or her name. Instead, Russell "muckraked" on more topics and wrote more exposés over a longer period of time than any of his more famous and well-known counterparts. See Miraldi, p. xi.
73   Miraldi writes that Russell learned about Phillips from a teacher named Wendell Phillips Stafford (no relation). Many years later, Russell wrote a book about Phillips; see Charles Edward Russell, *The Story of Wendell Phillips: Soldier of the Common Good* (Chicago: C.H. Kerr & Co., 1914).
74   Miraldi, p. 27, quoting Russell from an introduction he wrote to Caro

After two years in Vermont, Russell returned to Davenport to work for his father's newspaper. In 1884 he moved to Minnesota, where he became an editorial writer for the *St. Paul Pioneer Press*. In 1885, Russell moved to the *Minneapolis Tribune*, the city's leading political newspaper, to become its night editor; then, in 1886, he moved to the *Minneapolis Journal* to become its managing editor. After a few months, Russell left the *Journal* to manage the *Detroit Tribune* (a sister publication), but he only stayed for a short while. By the summer of 1886, Russell decided he wanted to find a reporting job in New York City.[75]

Russell was unable to secure a job as a reporter when he first arrived in New York City, so he turned to freelancing, writing stories about everything for some of the New York papers, and for the papers in Minneapolis and Detroit. After several months, Russell finally landed a full-time job with the *Commercial Advertiser*, a Republican paper that fit the "yellow journalism" trend of the time. Miraldi notes that Russell's style that developed during his months of freelancing showed an "alternating pattern of sensationalism and human interest balanced with enterprise and responsibility," and that this style would mark the rest of Russell's journalistic career.[76]

Russell spent about a year at the *Commercial Advertiser*. It was during this time that he gained meaningful insight into, and began to write about, the slums and the conditions of poverty in New York City. He reported on crime, general labor strife and a train strike. Russell believed that the cause of the crimes he reported was poverty and the horrible conditions in the city slums. When Russell proposed writing stories about the conditions of the poor in New York, the paper refused. Later, when the editors of the *Commercial Advertiser* wanted him to produce the names and addresses of strike leaders he had interviewed, Russell refused, knowing that the paper's loyalties were with the owners and not with labor. Russell would later write about his time at the *Commercial*

Lloyd, *Henry Demarest Lloyd, 1847–1903, A Biography, V. 1* (New York: G.P. Putnam's 1912), pp. vi, viii.

75   Miraldi, pp. 33–34.

76   Ibid, p. 40.

Advertiser: "the only education I ever had that amounted to anything was when I was a police reporter on the East Side of New York. One could learn there more about life as it really was than in any formal school of cloisters and dons that ever existed."[77]

In 1887, Joseph Pulitzer hired Russell to join the *New York World*. While at the *World*, Russell reported on a number of topics, but continued to develop a reputation as a crime reporter. He covered anarchist riots, hangings, the conditions at one of New York's most infamous prisons, Sing Sing, and he wrote profiles of Sing Sing's inmates. In 1889, when Russell left the *World* to join the *New York Herald*, he was one of the first journalists to cover execution by electrocution, a new experimental method for putting prisoners to death. Russell's reporting on electrocution was mostly positive, but years later he would become a critic of capital punishment and would eventually accept a position as vice president of the American League to Abolish Capital Punishment.[78]

Aside from covering crime, Russell also covered politics for the *Herald*. In 1892, the paper sent him to Minneapolis to report on the Republican National Convention (he had reported on the Republican National Convention in 1888 in Chicago for the *World*), then to Chicago to cover the 1892 Democratic National Convention. Grover Cleveland, the Democratic nominee for president in 1892, eventually would win the general election.

In covering the Democratic convention, Russell noticed the influence that William Whitney, a railroad magnate and former Secretary of the Navy, had on some of the Democratic delegations that were strongly opposed to Cleveland. After Whitney held private one-on-one meetings with delegates, support for Cleveland grew. Russell wondered how these people "magically transformed" into supporters, and privately suspected that Whitney was offering them money. Russell never wrote about this publicly and never had evidence to support his suspicions. Miraldi suggests that it was the coverage of the political conventions and the sense that bribes were changing hands within both parties that left Russell skeptical about not only politics, but also press reporting about it.

---

77   Ibid, pp. 42–43.
78   Ibid, pp. 48–50.

Did advertising buyouts or promises of purchased advertisements manipulate the press? This was an idea that Russell embraced later in his career and one he learned about especially when he became an editor [see chapters three and four]. In fact, Russell told of an incident, later in his career, when Whitney used his considerable power as a prominent New York businessman to kill a news story he did not want printed. But there is no evidence that commerce interfered with or stopped Russell from writing the reality of what he saw at the conventions. Perhaps Russell was reflecting another possibility: maybe it was the candidates and their handlers who carefully nurtured false impressions among the press, manipulating reporters and "spinning" accounts in ways that gullible reporters were accepting.[79]

In 1893, Russell took over as editor of the *Herald's* Brooklyn edition, where he reported on Brooklyn politics and corruption in city government. In December 1894, Russell moved back to Pulitzer's *New York World*, this time as the city editor, the third most important position at the paper. Pulitzer's paper and general philosophy was a good fit for Russell. According to newspaper historian Michael Schudson, "Pulitzer intended the *World* to provide both editorial leadership and news. ... He wanted the *World* to be 'both a daily school-house and a daily forum – both a daily teacher and a daily tribune.' This equal estimation of the editorial and news functions of the press was unusual in the late nineteenth century."[80]

Russell's belief that newspapers should hold elected officials accountable, and his general "disdain for excess wealth and unelected power," matched with Pulitzer's sense of purpose, opened the door for Russell to put his "principles into practice." The editorial pages under Russell's supervision "embraced the poor, mocked the blue-blooded wealthy, and crusaded especially against the emerging plutocratic monopolies that many felt were threatening democracy."[81]

Most notably, the topic of monopolies or "trusts," occupied many of

---

79   Ibid, p. 65.
80   Michael Schudson, *Discovering the News: A Social History of American Newspapers* (New York: Basic Books, 1978), p. 98.
81   Miraldi, p. 81.

the news and editorial pages of the *World* under Russell's leadership, publishing histories of how the trusts developed, arguing that the trusts bribed elected officials to impact the outcome of regulatory legislation, and demanding changes to the current situation. When the *World* was not successful in swaying public opinion (notably, it often was quite successful in shaping public opinion), it would sometimes become even more activist and work directly to affect change. In Russell's last months as city editor at the *World*, the paper went to court to seek injunctions against companies it believed were "grabbing" trolley and rail franchises in Manhattan, and against New York City government for its lack of upkeep of city streets. The *World* succeeded in gaining the injunctions, and embraced the spirit of the muckrakers of the early 20th century by working at all costs to expose what it perceived as injustice and abuses of wealth and power.[82]

In the summer of 1897, Russell left the *World* to join William Randolph Hearst's *New York Journal* as a managing editor. Hearst, according to historians, was one of the least scrupulous of the New York editors/publishers of the time, and was the most determined to build circulation at any cost. Hearst was one of the early proponents and purveyors of sensational news. "Every bizarre man-bites-dog story that came along – and some that were made up – hit the front pages. News accounts were often exaggerated to fit a story line." And while Hearst insisted that the stories in his newspaper were well written, they also had to be about a "subject matter embellishing a certain shock value or appealing to baser human emotions or eliciting mystery and intrigue almost beyond human comprehension."[83]

Where Russell and Hearst's sensibilities matched was in their shared belief that the citizens needed a voice to protect themselves from the growing power of corporate monopolies. This was very much in line with the mood of the American public at the time. And while many suggest that Hearst took the quality and credibility of journalism to new lows with his desire to sensationalize and sometimes make up the news, he was

---

82   Ibid, p. 85.
83   Schudson, p. 63; Miraldi, p. 93; Ben Procter, *William Randolph Hearst, The Early Years* (New York: Oxford University Press, 1998), pp. 137–138.

still respected by Russell because of his belief in the newspaper as an important progressive force. In 1900, when Hearst expanded to Chicago through the purchase of his third newspaper, the *Chicago American,* he named Russell publisher. Under Russell's leadership the paper carried on Hearst's tradition of both sensational and enlightening journalism. As Miraldi describes it, the *American's* "editorials were well-argued and generally progressive. Mix in a steady diet of crusades against local ignominies and a drumbeat of positive news about the Democratic Party and you have the *American* under Russell."[84]

Changing Directions

In 1901, Russell's wife died of typhoid fever. Soon after her death, Russell's health also started to decline. In the midst of a nervous break-down, Hearst gave Russell unlimited leave with pay, and for the next two years Russell took a break from journalism to focus on his health. Between 1900 and 1905, when Russell would publish his first series of muckraking articles, the practice of muckraking journalism had taken hold. Russell and his muckraking colleagues generally put forth the progressives' arguments of the time – that private capital was out of control, that wealthy industrial leaders were killing competition, and that the capitalistic system was largely to blame.

In Russell's first muckraking series he took on the meat packing industry, detailing in *Everybody's* magazine in 1905 the ways that the four large meatpacking companies had wiped out their competition. He profiled the four company owners and asserted of Jonathan Ogden Armour, the man who had inherited his father's meat packing business: "No more extraordinary figure has ever appeared in the world's commercial affairs, no man, not even Mr. Rockefeller, has conceived a commercial empire so dazzling."[85]

Russell's meat packing series appeared as socialist Upton Sinclair

---

84   Miraldi, p. 100.
85   Ibid, p. 111.

was living in Packingtown, and documenting the plight of the workers there for a piece he was writing for the socialist magazine *The Appeal to Reason*. Sinclair's work appeared a month after Russell's series in *Everybody's*, and then in 1906 it would be published as *The Jungle*, which had an enormous impact on the public.

Socialists were gaining in public acceptance in the early 1900s. The U.S. Socialist Party was founded in 1901 and attracted journalists, labor leaders, lawyers, educators and even some millionaires. Party founder Morris Hillquit noted in 1920 that the primary goal of "modern day" Socialism was "the abolition of private ownership in the vital sources and instruments of wealth production." Socialists challenged monopolies, championed labor and had serious misgivings about capitalism. Writes Hillquit: "The Socialists demand that the basic industries of the nation, the business of providing the necessaries of life, be conducted by the community for the benefit of its members. ... the enterprising captains of industry care little for the social value of the goods they produce. ... Socialism would substitute the prevailing method of private enterprise for individual profit by a system of social production for collective use."[86]

In 1908, Russell joined the Socialist Party. He would also continue to write exposé articles for various muckraking magazines.[87] After receiving a letter from a former Georgia prison inmate, Russell investigated Georgia's convict leasing system in which the prisons allowed private companies to pay the state for prisoner labor. Russell equated it to slavery. In addition to telling the personal story of one prisoner, Russell also noted that of Georgia's nearly 2,500 convicts, almost 1,900 were "contracted into servitude to various private persons and corporations," allowing the state to receive more than $350,000 in compensation for their work. "The whole thing is utterly and incurably and hopelessly evil," wrote Russell. "These profits are the sole returns from a system that multiplies crimi-

---

86   Morris Hillquit, *Present-Day Socialism* (Chicago: The Socialist Party of the United States, 1920), pp. 9, 21.
87   Russell freelanced between 1902 and 1915, and was an editor at *Hampton's*, *The Coming Nation* and *Pearson's* magazines. He also travelled extensively in Europe.

nals, breeds brutality, encourages crime, and puts upon one of the fairest states in the Union a hideous blot."[88]

The article generated a lot of publicity in Georgia because few knew the convict leasing system existed. The *Atlanta Journal-Constitution* wrote in an editorial that it opposed convict leasing and called for an end to it. Public pressure forced the Georgia legislature to take up the issue and in September 1908, the state reluctantly agreed to transfer prisoners to the state's counties to work on public roads, only allowing convict leasing to private contractors if counties could not find work for the prisoners. This effectively put an end to convict leasing because the state counties had ample need for the prisoners' labor. Although it did not have the same impact, Russell continued to write about the conditions at 14 federal and state prisons in a three-part series in 1909 published by *Hampton's* magazine. Miraldi writes that Russell's experiences in researching and writing about the prison system led him to consider not just exposing injustice, but to become a participant in social justice causes.[89]

This happened for the first time in 1909 when Russell worked with fellow socialist William Walling, fellow journalist Lincoln Steffens, social worker Mary White Ovington, black leader W.E.B. Du Bois, and progressive magazine editor Oswald Garrison Villard (grandson of famed abolitionist William Lloyd Garrison) to put out a call for the first National Negro Conference, which Russell was asked to chair. After the success of the first conference, the committee that lead the first meeting decided to hold a second conference and named their group the National Association for the Advancement of Colored People (NAACP). The NAACP asked a committee of 30 people, of which Russell was included, to serve as its board of directors. Their goals were to rid the nation of segregation, to protect the right to vote, and to ensure enforcement of the 14th and 15th Amendments. Generally speaking, the group's purpose was to improve the situation for black Americans, who were not only victims of segrega-

---

88   Charles Edward Russell, "A Burglar in the Making," *Everybody's*, June 1908, reprinted in Judith and William Serrin (Eds.), *Muckraking! The Journalism that Changed America* (New York: The New Press, 2002), pp. 343–346.
89   Miraldi, pp. 157–160.

tion, but were increasingly targets of various forms of violence including lynchings in both the North and the South.[90]

Russell's involvement in issues of racial justice is not surprising. As a child, his father, an abolitionist, told him it was a "sacred duty" to help slaves find freedom. His father did not believe in racial superiority, and taught him that blacks and whites were equal. Charles Edward Russell, in his years living among poor immigrants in New York City, came to believe that blacks and all non-natives were victims of discrimination, noting that class was really the problem. Even with this belief, he acknowledged that conditions for blacks required a "shield between the Negro and his oppressor," and he supported all efforts that advocated equal rights and opportunities for blacks.[91]

In 1910, Russell took his interest in participation in solving social problems to another level. He was chosen by the Socialist Party to run for governor of New York State. This would be one of four unsuccessful runs for political office by Russell. And while Russell's status as a socialist and a muckraking journalist was well known before he became a candidate for governor, what was less known beyond progressive and socialist circles was Russell's involvement in the founding of the NAACP. Most people knew Russell for his exposé articles about the beef trusts and for his 1908 book (a collection of articles), *Lawless Wealth*, that detailed how the wealthy in America built their fortunes.[92] He was hailed by many of the daily newspapers of the time as the "prince of muckrakers," and the conservative *New York Times* told its readers it should take Russell's candidacy seriously despite his status as a socialist. The *Times* called Russell an intellectual, and noted that it was odd he was a champion of the worker given that his only manual labor came "mostly at the typewriter."[93]

Russell's campaign for governor focused mostly on the message that

---

90   Miraldi, pp. 160–172; Lewis L. Gould, *America in the Progressive Era, 1890–1914* (Harlow, England: Pearson Education, 2001), pp. 49–50.

91   Miraldi, pp. 166–67.

92   Miraldi, pp. 173–175; Charles Edward Russell, *Lawless Wealth: The Origin of Some Great American Fortunes* (New York: B.W. Dodge & Company, 1908).

93   Miraldi, p. 173.

capitalism and competition were the primary causes of poverty and problems in the U.S. He specifically targeted issues of "poverty, slum housing,
the increased cost of living, the failure of regulation, corruption in government – and the concentration of power and wealth." Russell sought an
eight-hour workday, overtime pay, equal pay for men and women, a ban
on child labor, worker's compensation for on-the-job injuries, government-
funded pensions, lunch and breakfast programs for children in public
school, and a more rigorous civil service system. He also wanted to give
free land in upstate New York to people who lived in crowded urban areas;
he wanted local municipalities to assume control of most utilities; and,
he wanted the state to take control over some natural resources such as
timber and oil.[94]

Russell only managed to collect 4.4 percent of the votes in New York,
but he celebrated the fact that he drew so much public attention to his and
the socialists' views. In 1912, Russell again ran for Governor of New York
as the Socialist Party candidate; in 1913 he ran for Mayor of New York
City; and, in 1914 he ran as the socialist candidate for the U.S. Senate seat
in New York. Many expected Russell to be a contender for the Socialist
Party's presidential nomination in 1916, but Russell's views on the war
in Europe – of which he wrote and spoke about extensively in 1915 – led
to a public feud with the Socialist Party that ended with Russell leaving
the party. Russell agreed with socialists that it was capitalism that led to
the war in Europe, but he also believed that the monarchies in England
and Germany made democracy in those countries impossible. He criticized the practice of intermarriage among royalty, a practice he said was
condoned to keep lines of descent intact, and suggested that it resulted in
producing "lunatics and degenerates." His commentaries did not sit well
with German-born American socialists. Russell's "passion for democracy"
led him to focus more on German authoritarianism and its threat, and
less on commercialism. Russell's extensive travels through Europe in
1915 solidified his view that the U.S. needed to prepare to stave off the
threat that Germany presented to the U.S. by building up the American

---

94   Ibid, pp. 182–186.

military. When Russell said to a group of socialists in Philadelphia in 1915, "The world has refused to prevent war by abolishing the competition system [so] now we must fight," national party leaders condemned Russell's comments and told him that his speech disqualified him from the presidential nomination.[95]

In 1916, Russell returned to journalism, serving as a war correspondent for the Newspaper Enterprise Association, a subsidiary of the Scripps-Howard Newspapers. His belief in the need for American intervention intensified, partially because of the human atrocities and horrors he witnessed in the war zones. Russell also believed that the war threatened democracy around the world, and the only way to save democracy was for the U.S. to step in. He was not the only socialist who felt this way, and at the Socialist Party convention in 1916 he and others formally broke with the party over their differing views. As Miraldi explains it

> Russell's basic principle was simple: without democracy, there could not be socialism. "The world is rent with the greatest of all struggles between the opposing principles of democracy and autocracy. The future of the democratic cause everywhere depends upon the issue," he declared. By not opposing Germany, the party was betraying "the interests of the working class." In closing, he said, "Between men of these convictions and men that feel their first loyalty is to monarchy and Germany there can be no association."[96]

Russell and others who were like-minded became known as the pro-war socialists. In addition to Russell, Upton Sinclair, Chester M. Wright, the editor of the *New York Call*, presidential candidate Allan Benson, and author William Ghent, among others, resigned from the party over the war issue.

Soon after leaving the party, Russell would undertake a diplomatic mission at the invitation of President Woodrow Wilson. The goal of the mission was to convince Russia to stay with the American alliance in

---

95   Ibid, p. 239.
96   Ibid, pp. 242–243.

fighting the Germans. Three weeks before the U.S. entered the war, the Russian people revolted, toppling the czar. On April 6, 1917, the day the U.S. formally entered the war, Wilson sent a message to Russia welcoming it as the world's newest democracy and letting the country know that a political and economic relationship with the U.S. was welcome. Russell's group was really engaged in "propaganda work."[97]

Toward the end of 1917, Russell wrote a book about Russia and participated in a lecture tour organized by the newly formed Committee for Public Information (CPI). President Wilson created this committee to generate support for the war, and he hired former muckraking editor George Creel to head the CPI. Many former journalists worked for the CPI, which oversaw and executed a sweeping domestic propaganda campaign. By the spring of 1918, Russell was asked to head the CPI's publicity office in England.[98]

In the years after World War I, Russell wrote 17 books. Many were biographies and histories. In 1920, he won the Pulitzer Prize for his book about the Nonpartisan League. He died in 1941, remembered mostly as a journalist who used his writing to affect social and political change. His legacy as a leader within the NAACP was also highlighted in some of his obituaries. In a resolution honoring Russell after he died, the Washington, D.C. branch of the NAACP wrote, "we rededicate ourselves to the practical establishment of those principles for which literally he gave his long and useful life; and that we determine, separately and jointly, not to rest until his ideas and ideals of justice are a part of the daily workings of the District and our Nation."[99]

---

97   Ibid, pp. 245-250.
98   Schudson, p. 142; Miraldi, p. 255.
99   "Charles Edward Russell," *the Crisis* (September, 1941), p. 301.

Chapter 3

Who Controls the Newspaper?

In 21st century American journalism, the presence of advertising is so prevalent and common, people notice its absence perhaps more than its presence. This wasn't always the case. The newspaper became a truly commercial enterprise in the 19th century. As historian Thomas Leonard notes, "alarms sounded after the Civil War" when advertising became the primary source of revenue for newspapers, replacing payments from readers who either subscribed or purchased newspapers at the newsstands.[100] During the 1880s, the ratio of news content compared to advertising content shrank from 70–30 to 50–50. In 1880, money from advertising made up about 44 percent of a newspaper's total income. By 1900, advertising revenue comprised 55 percent. It was also in the late 19th century that advertising developed as a separate business – N.W. Ayer and Son became the first modern advertising agency, opening for business in 1875.[101]

Charles Edward Russell was among the many journalists of the late 19th and early 20th century who witnessed the profound and increasing influence advertising had on news content. In a 1914 memoir, Russell called the newspaper an "appendage of the department store," in reference to the largest advertiser for most city papers at the end of the 19th century.[102] Leonard notes, "the stories killed by advertisers became part

---

100   Thomas Leonard, *News for All, America's Coming-of-Age with the Press* (New York: Oxford University Press, 1995), p. 188.

101   Michael Schudson, *Discovering the News: A Social History of American Newspapers* (New York: Basic Books, 1978), p. 93.

102   Charles Edward Russell, *These Shifting Scenes* (New York: Hodder & Stoughton, George H. Doran, Co., 1914), p. 309.

of the talk of the trade," and by 1912, journalists like Russell began more publicly denouncing and exposing the influence advertising had on the news. In 1919, famous muckraking novelist Upton Sinclair wrote *The Brass Check*, which was "a tome on the prostitution of the press," and detailed many instances of advertisers exerting their influence over newspapers to censor or alter news reporting.[103] In a brief letter Sinclair published to introduce the book, a friend acknowledged Sinclair's courage "to attack the monster, the new Minotaur, to which the entire world renders tribute: the Press."[104]

Russell, though, had attacked the new Minotaur several years earlier in a series of articles that *Pearson Magazine* published in 1914. According to a short profile about the magazine that appeared in the *New York Times* in 1901, *Pearson's* was first established in the U.S. in 1899, and grew rapidly in circulation. The *Times*, considered a conservative paper in the early 20th century, was also a paper that resisted efforts to sensationalize its news – attributed the magazine's success to "the good judgment shown in the selection of the material to be found in the magazine. ... The magazine is prepared to treat all the leading subjects of human interest as they present themselves."[105] Some historians have called *Pearson's* a muckraking magazine while under the editorship of Arthur W. Little and Frank Harris; the U.S. version of the publication folded in 1925.

The article re-published below is the first in the series written by Russell, and focuses on the impact of advertising on the news and on newspaper ownership. The series as a whole took on the problems of advertiser influence, newspaper ownership, media monopolies, efforts to shut down the muckraking magazines, and efforts by corporations to unduly influence public thought and opinion through the traveling lecture series' of the time (see chapter four). Russell wrote for *Pearson's* from 1913–1917.

---

103   Leonard, p. 188; See also Upton Sinclair, *The Brass Check: A Study of American Journalism* (Pasadena Calif.: Upton Sinclair, 1920).
104   Sinclair, p. 3.
105   "Pearson's Magazine," *New York Times*, Nov. 23, 1901.

Pearson Magazine's preface to Russell's article:

The plain truth about the effectual control of our newspapers is here explained by Mr. Russell. Mr. Russell knows. He has been everything on a newspaper from cub reporter to city editor. He has been in the business for 30 years. You probably no longer care for editorials or certainly you are not much influenced by them. You are influenced by the news. You want to know what's going on and you will form your own opinion. You do not care much what some editor thinks about things. You will do your own thinking. That's fine. That's the right way. The only trouble about it is that the men who control the newspapers know it and you do not get the whole truth in the news. You get news cleverly perverted to suit certain ends and consequently your opinion of things is often very far from what it would be if you knew the real story. Every newspaper man knows this. Here's where you can learn it. Here's the truth about how newspapers are made, told by a man who for many years helped to make them. This is the truth from the inside.

The Keeping of the Kept Press
By Charles Edward Russell[106]

In the years when I was city editor of the *New York World* I was on terms of confidential intimacy with the late Joseph Pulitzer (the creator of the great *World* property) and observed that one source of his pride in his newspaper was his belief that its news columns were absolutely unbiased.

"Do the fighting in the editorial columns," Mr. Pulitzer would say. "Keep the news always uncolored. Let the news columns invariably treat our opponents even better than our friends. Never tolerate the least discrimination against men or causes that we attack editorially. Never mix the news policy with the editorial policy."

---

106   Charles Edward Russell, "The Keeping of the Kept Press," *Pearson's Magazine* (vol. 31, no. 1, January, 1914).

Even then Mr. Pulitzer's confidence in this rule of practice was larger than it would have been but for the cruel misfortune that deprived him of the pleasure of reading his newspaper. Before he died his doctrine of news independence had become largely a tradition. To-day it amounts scarcely to a reminiscence – in the office of his newspaper, or, practically speaking, of any other.

Here is beyond all comparison the most tremendous force in modern life, as subtle as it is overwhelming and irresistible, and almost no attention is paid to it or to the revolutions it is working.

Every day in the year some thousands of newspapers are not so much (in the old phrase) moulding public opinion as perverting it and poisoning it. Often unconsciously; sometimes consciously and unwillingly; but always under the pressure of a condition so inexorable that it leaves no choice.

A great and wonderful change has come over the newspaper business in the last thirty years. The editor and the writer of editorials have abdicated. The real control of public thought and action lies now in the pencils of the reporter and of the writer of head-lines.

With few exceptions, nobody now reads or cares for an editorial. The mere fact that it is an expression of opinion kills all interest in the average reader. The American public no longer gives a hoot for anybody's opinions; it has definitely formed the habit of making its own. No man says now, "I see that the editor of the *Tribune* thinks so and so." What the newspaper reader says is, "I see that President Wilson has signed the tariff bill," whereupon he launches into an opinion that is to him much better than the opinion of any editor on earth.

Here is a group of newspapers that together will have to-morrow, let us say, ten million readers. Here is an event that all will describe. Half a dozen words added to their report of it will create in the mind of every reader a certain impression upon which ten million opinions will assuredly be based. Suppose what is added is false, malicious, or perverted with design toward a certain end. No reader will know that such is the case. Then here are ten million false opinions generated in a moment of time, certain to endure, extremely likely to fructify in some action, and all, it may be, making for evil.

I will give one little example from recent news.

When Mrs. Emmeline Pankhurst, the militant suffragist of England, landed at New York last October, the local immigration officers detained her and ordered her to be deported on the ground that she had been convicted of a crime "involving moral turpitude." Her offense, or alleged offense, was that she had, in the judgment of an English court, "incited some one to the destruction of property." She had done this, if at all, in the course of an agitation to reform the election laws of England, and the only question that could be considered, was whether this was a "crime involving moral turpitude," or whether it was a political offense, for which our laws have never debarred anyone from landing upon our shores.

The immigration officers at New York held, or said they held, the "moral turpitude" ideal. They had, in fact, decided to exclude Mrs. Pankhurst before she had sailed from the other side. An appeal was taken to the authorities at Washington. These reversed the finding of the local board and allowed Mrs. Pankhurst to land.

A New York newspaper in its Washington correspondence reporting this reversal, managed with great skill and art to convey the impression that before he would allow her to land President Wilson had exacted from Mrs. Pankhurst a pledge that she would not preach militancy in the United States. Observe that the correspondent did not assert this, for such an assertion would be preposterous. President Wilson would have no more right to exact such a pledge than he would have to exact a pledge that Mrs. Pankhurst should not wear false hair. But by a deft weaving of words the dispatch was so manipulated as to create such an impression in the mind of any reader not conversant with the law and the nature of our proceedings.

The newspaper that performed this adroit trick is strongly opposed to woman suffrage.

The leading London newspapers maintain in New York correspondents that are Englishmen and unfamiliar with American laws and methods. These journals are likewise strongly opposed to woman suffrage.

Their correspondents in New York seized upon the idea skillfully insinuated in this Washington dispatch and cabled it to London as a fact.

Two nights later, Mr. Lloyd George, Chancellor of the English Exchequer, speaking at Swindon in his country, gleefully told his audience that President Wilson had exacted this pledge and pointed to it as an endorsement of the position of the English government toward the suffragists. To-day probably nine-tenths of the English people firmly believe that the United States government would not allow Mrs. Pankhurst to land until she had promised not to speak about militancy. They will always think so.

Mr. Lloyd George's remarks were cabled back to this country by the Associated Press and printed in nearly all the American newspapers. As no way exists to counteract such things an immense number of Americans have also imbibed the same notion about the proceedings in the Pankhurst case and it will never be dislodged from their minds.

The next time an advocate of an unpopular cause arrives on our shores, a certain part of the public will demand that he be gagged in advance. "The government did it in the case of Mrs. Pankhurst, you know."

In the presence of a power so tremendous as this and so absolutely irresponsible and boundless, all thoughtful men must be appalled.

When next we reflect that such perversions of fact occur every day and many times a day, that in most instances they are never uncovered, that they are never corrected, that all of us from our newspaper reading are daily absorbing impressions any one of which may have been as artfully doctored and tinctured with poison as this one dispatch I have mentioned, the glimpse thus afforded of the real governing power of this world and the uses to which it may be put is enough to make us all gasp.

Then if we contemplate the next great fact, which is that this incalculable power is now for the most part consciously swayed and directed in behalf of the most reactionary influences in American life, we can well understand why we are sociologically the most backward nation on earth and why it is absurd to refer to the government at Washington as of any real potency or otherwise than as a mere figurehead.

The real government lies in the hands of the men that control the news columns of our daily journals.

And who are they?

The men that also control our great industries, railroads and financial enterprises.

That being the case, what else would you expect but backwardness?

At my statement of the real nature of the real control now exerted upon our newspapers many conscientious but uninformed journalists will cry out in protest. Their weekly wages are paid (without their knowledge) by exactly this power and they daily serve (without their knowledge) exactly this power, but so strong upon them is the delusion of professional pride that they will deny what they could prove for themselves if they would once read facts with their eyes and not with their prejudices.

Let's see then how this matter really stands.

The very aorta of every considerable enterprise, whether a newspaper or anything else, is, of course, its connection with a ready money supply.

The money supply of this country is now dominated by two harmonious groups of capitalists, who together own or control about one-third of the total wealth of the United States.

Practically speaking, every great manufacturing or mercantile enterprise, if it is not owned directly or indirectly by these groups, is still at their mercy. They control the money supply that is its arterial life. Consequently you might say that business is now carried on under their license. As a rule they are rather easy masters of the situation; they neither exact nor interfere unreasonably; but there is one point about which they are exceedingly sensitive and exceedingly insistent. It is that they shall not be criticized in the public press nor subjected to comment likely to interfere with their plans.

To that end it is absolutely necessary to them that they shall control or dominate the newspapers and periodicals.

In three ways these influences have erected in America a censorship of the daily press that in plain terms is as strict as any government censorship ever established in Russia or Spain.

This will astonish you only if you have never had occasion to look into the subject with unprejudiced eyes. Contemplate the facts.

Certain newspapers they own outright.

Certain newspapers they control through business, social and personal relations.

All the newspapers they gag through the irresistible medium of the advertising business.

Nearly every American newspaper is manufactured at a loss.

It sounds like insanity, but it is a truth, nevertheless. The price received for a single copy does not ordinarily pay for the white paper it is printed upon, to say nothing of the ink, press work, overhead charges, or anything else.

To meet this heavy deficit and to make above it any kind of a profit, the one chance is in the advertising.

Advertisements the newspaper must have and plenty of them or it goes under.

The bulk of the display advertising is supplied by the department stores.

The department stores withhold their advertising from any newspaper with the news conduct of which they are dissatisfied or from one that for any reason they do not like.

All the department stores are now connected with the great Central Financial Interests. Some are owned outright and some have the money lariat about their necks.

What do your denials look like now?

The first result is that not one item of news of which these Interests seriously disapprove can be published in any of these newspapers.

The next is that not one cause, movement, reform, betterment or political party that these Interests fear or greatly oppose can have from these journals anything but ridicule, misrepresentation, lies, slanders, reckless inventions, or the absolute suppression of its news.

Every genuine reform and social advance must be hateful to these interests because they hold their vast and autocratic power only by a reversion to practical feudalism.

All of these results are achieved through the control of the news column and most effectively through the control of the very publications that make the most pretense of progressive or even radical sympathies.

This is the most vicious phase of the whole vicious situation.

Frankly reactionary and Bourbon journals like the *New York Times*,

the *Washington Post*, the *Chicago Inter Ocean*, the *Los Angeles Times* and
the *San Francisco Chronicle* do no harm at any time in their editorial
column. It is a wonderful provision of divine wisdom and one we cannot
too much admire that the editorial mind dull enough to be reactionary is
likewise so dull in its utterances that nobody can read them. The editorials in papers of this class are the exclusive perusal of the proofreader,
who is hired for the job and usually, on just grounds, complaining of
underpayment.

But a journal like the *New York World* or the *Chicago Tribune* is a
different proposition. The mere fact that at intervals, apparently calcu-
lated, it professes progressive sentiments, denounces some extravagance
of the System, or says something about democracy and the people does the
harm. For when under the cover of such pretensions it slips the poisoned
dagger into some movement or cause of genuine worth the poison is of
double power and does its worst work.

The *World*, for instance, with loud acclaim will print an editorial
denouncing the New Haven railroad for killing so many people. Then it
will slip over a series of articles declaring that there are no slums and no
poverty in America, praising the American railroad system as the best
ever known, turning the woman's movement to ridicule or misrepresenting
some meeting. Let the drivers for the contractors that handle the federal
mails go on a strike for better conditions and decent treatment and the
World hands them this:

THE STUPIDITY OF STRIKES

A better object-lesson of the stupidity and recklessness of strikes
could hardly be afforded than in that of the mail-van chauffeurs in
lower Manhattan yesterday.

Only about 125 men were concerned. In a quarrel involving the
hours and wages of this mere handful they were willing to tie up the
mail service of the Nation; lower New York handles not only a very large
part of the domestic mail of the entire country but the great majority
of all the letters from foreign nations pass through it.

In almost every strike the public is the chief loser; in every strike the worst and not the best method of settling the questions at dispute is resorted to. But it is not often that the interests of non-combatants are so overwhelmingly disproportionate to the petty quarrel in progress.

And when two vans driven by strike-breakers run over and kill citizens the *World* in its news columns most carefully cuts out any reference to the strike-breakers and every suggestion that a strike was in progress.

Or say that a shop girl commits suicide because she is wearied of the struggle to keep herself alive on the miserable pittance she is able to earn. The *World* promptly comes to the front with a dose of its compound poison as this:

> "It is not to be assumed that it was the twenty cent dinners that made the poverty unbearable. Thousands of people have such dinners not for six months only but for years, yet live not unhappily. There are families whose income hardly exceeds the amount earned by this impatient girl; yet in their homes there is vitality enough to provide the joy of life even when the dinner is scant and the menu monotonous.
>
> ...There are some people who make too large a demand upon fortune. Fixing their eyes upon the standards of living flaunted by the rich, they measure their requirements by their desires. Such persons are easily affected by outside influences, and perhaps in this case the recent discussions, more often silly than wise, concerning the relations of wages to vice, may have made this girl more susceptible than usual to the depressing effects of cheap dinners."

Which neatly informs the poor that they are to be patient in the lot to which society has consigned them and at the same time does a good piece of lackey service for the department stores that furnish the advertising.

The merchants are against this "silly" discussion of the relations of low wages to vice and so the faithful *World* takes a hack at it and shows how loyal it is to the gentlemen that pay its board.

In all the newspapers, whether frankly reactionary or ostensibly progressive, the handling of the news does the most effective work for evil. Often a mere headline on an item is all that is needed. Many persons read only the headlines; all readers are influenced by them.

A few months ago an elderly man at Wilmington, Delaware, committed suicide. Some domestic troubles had afflicted him and he had lost money in stocks, particularly express stocks. The *New York Times* is opposed to the parcels post, as it is opposed to everything that would interfere with railroad graft. It put over this item a headline adroitly conveying the impression that the unfortunate man had been driven to suicide by the parcels post.

Against the injuries wrought by News Perversion no individual and no cause has protection and for such injuries there is no redress. The newspapers that perpetrate these things will not correct them, no matter how much harm they do.

In 1908 *Everybody's Magazine* published an article about the late Governor John A. Johnson of Minnesota. It contained an interview with Governor Johnson, all of which was submitted to him before publication and then printed with his corrections and approval. When it appeared a news agency sent out from St. Paul a story that Governor Johnson had denounced the interview a fake. Hundreds of papers printed this story prominently and many gave it editorial comment to the injury of the writer and the magazine. Governor Johnson's attention being called to the fact that he could not deny an interview that he had authorized, revised, and approved, he declared that he had never denied it nor thought of denying it. This statement with an explanation of the facts was sent to sixteen newspapers that had printed the denial story on their first pages. Not one of them would print the correction.

At that time the magazine was regarded as dangerously radical; so was the interviewer; and to swat both was deemed a meet service for our Overlords.

Six or seven years ago a man that had been engaged to some extent in attacking organized wealth and the central interests was invited to address the men's club at one of the great New York churches. A corps commander on the *New York Sun* selected his cleverest writer and sent him to report the address with instructions to ridicule the speaker. When the reporter returned the editor in charge said:

"Well, can you give us one of your snappy stories, sarcastic and ridiculing, and all that?

"There wasn't anything to ridicule," said the reporter.

"Why not? What did he talk about?"

"The housing of the poor."

"Oh, well, write a stickful about the meeting and just add a line that – muckraked."

For reasons I have indicated the Central Interests are opposed to woman suffrage. Consequently the newspapers of New York are generally opposed to woman suffrage. When the Pankhurst meeting was held in Madison Square Garden only one newspaper told the truth about it; all the rest monstrously distorted or concealed the facts, and covered what was really an impressive occasion with choice specimens of this hee-haw humor. Of them all the most conspicuous offender was the *New York Times*, which printed a report containing misstatements too gross that they awakened an unusual protest among a public long inured to such things. One of the editors of the *Times* was interrogated over the telephone and in reply to a complaint remarked illuminatingly;

"Oh well, you can't expect a woman suffrage meeting to be reported seriously, you know."

One of the misstatements was of a peculiarly flagrant and injurious character. Letters were written to the *Times* asking for a correction of this falsehood. No attention was paid to these requests. An old and warm personal friend of the city editor wrote to him remonstrating against these manifest wrongs. No reply was returned to his letter.

In view of these facts it may be thought that one trying to cling to the belief that these things are not deliberate and intentioned will have many difficulties.

Some years ago when I was an executive in the Hearst organization,

Brisbane[107] went to Europe for his vacation and the task of writing the editorials for the *Evening Journal* fell upon me. Here are some of the incidents that followed:

One day I made in an editorial a plea for the municipal ownership and operation of public utilities, among them, if I remember rightly, the subway then under construction. The next day in came one of the advertising men with a face longer than the moral law. He said:

> "I can't get any business for this paper if it publishes articles like this. Don't you know Mr. --- at Wanamaker's is dead against this sort of thing?"

A few days later I happened to refer incidentally to a bill then pending for the benefit of the clerks in the department stores. Two advertising men hopped in and informed me that I was ruining the paper.

An Englishman named Hart came to New York about that time on a mission to abate the national dyspepsia by reforming our bread. He was a purely altruistic old philosopher and had not profit from his theories, some of which were exceedingly interesting. I allowed him to write for us a little piece on elementary dietetics in the course of which he somewhat disparaged the use of cereal breakfast foods.

The next day I was lugubriously informed that I had knocked $100,000 a year (or some such sum) from the advertising revenues of the *Journal*. The manufacturers of "Somebody's Heavenly Mush for Breakfast" had spied poor old Mr. Hart's reference and withdrawn all their advertising. The idea appeared to be that we must stand by mush whether it was good for us or not. Mush advertised.

Not long after a casual mention of the efforts of the Merchants' Association to increase the troubles of travelers returning from abroad came

---

107   Russell is referring to Arthur Brisbane, one of the most famous American newspaper editors of the early 20th century. Russell worked with Brisbane at the *New York World*, which at the time was owned by Joseph Pulitzer. Later, Russell and Brisbane worked together at the *New York Evening Journal*, owned by William Randolph Hearst.

near to causing a riot in the office. Finally I said in despair to one of the advertising men:

> "Well, what on earth can I write about?
> He brightened visibly.
> "I'll tell you," says he, "write something cracking up golf. Mr.
> --- of Macy's is woozy about golf."

I was glad when Brisbane came home.

He himself was often in hot water. Once he wrote an editorial explaining on scientific grounds how the wearing of stiff hats produces baldness and advising his readers to wear soft hats. When this came out the dealers and department stores that had laid in seasonable stocks of stiff hats went up into the air. I saw a group of advertising men outside Brisbane's door, waiting for him, and it seemed likely that some of them would perish of apoplexy.

Since then the lines have been still more closely drawn, not only in New York but everywhere. When the Illinois Vice Commission last winter started to rip up the mistreatment of department store girls only one newspaper in Chicago dared to print an unbiased account of the testimony. Most of the others were industriously engaged in trying to discredit the inquiry from the moment it turned its attention to the great advertisers. One of them even put up a job by which women of the underworld were supposed to write letters declaring that low wages and bad living conditions never drove any woman to prostitution but women turned prostitutes because they deliberately preferred that kind of a life. Beyond this in service to the masters it does not seem humanly possible to go, but the fabrication was joyously taken up by newspapers all about the country and pointed to as conclusive proof that there is nothing wrong about our noble department stores, fountains of so much good advertising.

In New York one editorial writer on a morning paper slipped in a three-line paragraph suggesting that the girls from the stores be called no less than their employers to testify to the conditions of their employment. He received at once a savage warning from his superior. The

Merchants' Association didn't like that sort of thing, he was told. A full chorus of obedient newspapers got the signal and started off on this matter of the connection between low wages and vice to show that it did not exist. Every day they printed columns of interviews with all persons that could be induced to support this view, and every day they conscientiously suppressed everything that would bear a contrary significance.

The department store censor had pulled the string.

In Philadelphia the greatest advertiser is the Wanamaker house. Only one Philadelphia paper has reported the troubles of that house with the United States customs service, although that story was legitimate news if any such was ever on earth.

In New York a league that exists for the purpose of purifying and elevating the advertising business prosecuted a famous store for advertising one kind of furs and selling another. The case was novel and of great interest, but not a New York newspaper would print a line about the proceedings, even when the case came to trial and a verdict was rendered. The store was a heavy advertiser.

All kinds of accidents and misadventures have occurred in the department stores and have been suppressed in the daily journals. The only news about a department store that gets by is a story about the arrest of a shop-lifter and the efficient work of the store detective. This is printed for the sake of the deterrent effect upon other thieves.

It is the string again.

When I was engaged in newspaper work the strings were so many and pulled from so many different directions that every executive was often puzzled how to proceed. Every night editor's desk was furnished with a long and elaborate list of office "Don'ts," but even these were not always enough to steer by. "Don't mention" this and "Don't print anything about" that and "Don't antagonize" the other were the burden of these instructions, and at all times hung over us the terror of the advertiser and the threat of "the hunch." "Why, that firm is one of our advertisers" was enough at any time to spike any story. As for "the hunch," that was a word quietly passed along the line without comment or elaboration that it was deemed wise to bear lightly upon this event or take a strong position about that, both being related to the advertising receipts or the financial powers that be.

All of these conditions are far worse today. It is now the accepted doctrine that newspapers shall boom in their news columns the thing the advertisers are interested in and suppress all subjects to which advertisers are opposed.

The fact is, the position of any editor, managing editor or city editor in New York to-day is merely nominal. The real editors are the advertisers. And back of them the Central Financial Interests.

Under this able editorship you are not likely to learn from your press one fact that the Central Interests do not wish you to learn.

To be sure, some exceptions exist to these general conditions. For example I ought in fairness to say here that the newspapers owned, controlled or largely influenced by what is called the Scripps-McRae combination are not to be included with the subjugated. Mr. Scripps is very wealthy, very independent, and very far-sighted. He has solved for himself the problem of newspaper freedom by producing a peculiar but still successful newspaper inside of the manufacturing cost. Having his own capital the banks cannot reach him and being independent of advertising he cares naught for the department stores. He has even achieved that seemingly impossible feat of making a successful newspaper without any advertising of any kind.

Besides these a very few struggling journals like the *New York Call* printed by workingmen's cooperative associations contend against the tide. They are supported from the scanty earnings of toilers and are free but not strong enough to make headway.

I ought also to single out a paper like the *San Francisco Bulletin*, which under the command of men of unusual courage and independence continues for a time to print what it pleases and defy the censor. But the case of the *Bulletin* is also the aptest illustration of these general truths. For years it has been uncontrolled and uncontrollable, one of its conspicuous offenses being to print regularly the news of the Socialist movement, which the Central Interests have put on their "Don't Mention" list. Failing in every attempt to buy, bribe or bully the *Bulletin* and also in a well-planned attempt to crush it by withdrawing its advertising, the Interests have now combined to overwhelm and silence it with a competitor supplied with unlimited means.

In one way or another they will still try to get what they want.

Among the results of the news censorship they establish is this, that communities are deprived incidentally of knowledge of many things that would be useful to them and things at the same time that are not really of a nature treasonable to the Overlords.

For example, the city of New York is confronted with many and puzzling problems in its government and affairs – problems of wise management and not in any way related to the supremacy of the Traction Trust and the Morgan Group. Other cities in this country have dealt with the same problems; some have solved them. Two mayors of cities that by experiment have found practical solutions for these troubles came to New York in October and at Carnegie Hall related to a great audience the experiences and successes of their respective communities. The occasion was of great and unusual interest. Ordinarily it would have been reported fully in all the New York newspapers. This time not one of them so much as mentioned it. The two mayors belonged to a movement that the Merchants' Association and the Central Interests have put on the black list. The "hunch" had gone out that under no conditions was that movement to be so much as mentioned and as usual the "hunch" was faithfully obeyed. Some of the contortions, twistings and lying that obedience involved were vastly entertaining to philosophers but there appeared no treason in the realm of the long green.

Or take for another example the daily financial and business news. If there is anything about which people might be supposed to have a right to know it is the condition of business – particularly in a "business nation" you know. But in seven years scarcely one newspaper in the United States has reported accurately the state of business in or out of Wall Street whenever such a report would show any considerable depression. In all important offices the necessity of maintaining a fictitious cheerfulness about the business situation is now so well recognized that such doctored reports are no longer regarded as faking; they are as much a part of the day's work as putting the paper to press.

Who, for instance, reading the daily Wall Street market reports would suspect that for months there has been no Wall Street market and that the reported sales are "wash" or else trading back and forth among the houses? Yet such is the fact. Every Wall Street man knows well enough that the American public has not been in Wall Street any more than it has been in Siam, and that consequently the quotations and comment daily printed are so much bosh; but not one of them would be allowed to say this in the columns of his newspaper. The censor wouldn't like it.

To say these things seems to be fraught with some danger – or at least to anyone that these influences can get at. Two years ago Senator LaFollette, in a celebrated speech at Philadelphia, ventured to lay bare something of the actual condition of the American press and the press took upon him a memorable revenge. I have his speech before me now. He said no word that was not true; he made no assertion that was extravagant; he carried moderation so far in his utterances that he seemed to be trying studiously to understate the facts. And yet from the press you would have thought that it was the speech of a madman. As if at a signal the newspapers leaped upon him and covered him with abuse misrepresentation, ridicule and filth. They even succeeded in creating the impression that this man, whose strongest beverage is buttermilk, was intoxicated. They started and spread industriously the story that because of this speech he had withdrawn from the presidential race; they sought subtly to undermine the respect in which he had been held by the masses of the people; and it is doubtful if in his lifetime he will recover from the injuries that were wrought upon him because he told the truth about the kept press of America.

No man has any protection against these things and no redress when they have been practiced upon him. Let him once be black-listed by the Merchants' Association or the Central Interests, let him attack Thomas Fortune Ryan or criticize August Belmont and he may be shot at from any convenient angle. The ferocity with which Colonel William N. Amory, the first exposer of the New York traction swindle, has been pursued is a sufficient illustration of this fact.

One hopeful sign is that the vast evils of a kept press are beginning to appeal to legislators, although laws they are passing to deal with the situation are only ridiculous. One of the latest requires newspapers to make public something of their ownership with the purpose of detecting the real control. No remedy could be feebler, for to hide the real owner-ship through dummies and mortgages or concealed loans is ever a thing of childish simplicity, and what then becomes of the law?

But speaking of the ownership of newspapers, here is a point to be considered. At the outset of this chapter we mentioned direct ownership as one of the ways in which control was established for the good of the Interests and the suppression of news. This is plainly enough exempli-fied by the myriad journals all about the country owned directly by the traction and electric combination that controls the street railroads of so many cities. They of course do faithful service to their owners. But how another kind of ownership works in practice may be gathered from this information concerning the newspapers of New York. It may be an owner-ship not reflected in the stock-books nor in other records of transactions; it may even be indefinable in terms of dollars; and yet be none the less effective in establishing the control that is the last word.

Two are owned by Mr. James Gordon Bennett.

Mr. Bennett is enormously rich and lives in Paris, whence he directs his journals in the interest of British and other aristocracy.

One is owned by Mr. Frank A. Munsey.

Mr. Munsey is one of the largest owners of the United States Steel Corporation, commonly known as the Steel Trust.

One is owned by the D. O. Mills estate.

This estate is one of the largest and most important in New York and is heavily interested in Wall Street.

Two are owned by the Pulitzer estate.

I do not know how the funds of this wealthy estate are at present invested, but a few years ago it held large quantities of railroad and telegraph stocks. A man may be bribed with his own money as easily and as effectively as with another man's.

One is owned by August Belmont.

Mr. Belmont is the active head of the great traction Interests of New York.

One is owned by Mr. George W. Perkins.

Mr. Perkins is the chief influence in the Harvester Trust and heavily interested in Cincinnati, Hamilton & Dayton and other railroads. He was formerly a partner in the house of Morgan & Co.

One is owned by the Mark Hopkins estate.

Mr. Hopkins was one of the Big Four that reaped the rich harvest of the Pacific railroad deals with the government.

One is owned by William Rockefeller.

Mr. Rockefeller is now the active influence in Standard Oil.

Two are owned by Mr. Hearst.

To show how futile are regulative laws when they attempt to deal with such a situation, some of the gentlemen above named could swear each that he has not now and never had one dollar invested in any newspaper on earth. Which would be perfectly true. And yet in each case he is the real power because directly or indirectly he has furnished the funds and whatever the stock books might show to investigators he holds the strings of actual influence.

The continuation of such a condition as has been here outlined is unthinkable if we are to make any progress or preserve even the semblance of a democracy. A democracy has no other foundation than the intelligent participation by its citizens in their government. The citizens of the United States cannot participate intelligently in their government for the reason that they are never allowed to know the truth about their affairs. Instead of a democracy we have here a kind of concealed autocracy of the Central Interests with the kept press as its most powerful, efficient, ready instrument in maintaining an absolute control.

The remedy for such a situation is not in any law. A law that would compel every newspaper to correct on demand its gravely injurious falsehoods would be a palliative but no cure. There can be no cure for the kept press until there ceases to be a power sufficiently great and sufficiently interested to keep on keeping the press.

How can that be achieved so long as the vast majority of the people are deprived of knowledge of the facts that really concern them?

To that question the only answer that we must steadfastly support, further and develop the few publications we now have that are not under the advertising lasso and can therefore tell the truth.

Without a free press other free institutions are impossible and so long as nineteenths of the newspapers are kept as ours are kept to speak of a free press is a mere mockery.

• • •

The Future of the Muckraking Magazines

Russell wasn't only concerned about the future of newspapers. In February 1914, he published his follow-up to "The Keeping of the Kept Press" with an article entitled "The Magazine Soft Pedal," that promoted his theory that "a conspiracy existed to put the muckraking magazines out of business."[108] According to Russell biographer Robert Miraldi, well-

---

108   Robert Miraldi, *The Pen is Mightier: The Muckraking Life of Charles Edward Russell* (New York, Palgrave MacMillan, 2003), p. 193.

known journalist and public thinker Walter Lippmann and others agreed with Russell that a vast corporate conspiracy was to blame for the closure of many muckraking magazines between 1908 and 1915.[109] Miraldi suggests that not enough evidence exists to fully support Russell's claim in the sense that "The powerful banker J.P. Morgan did not convene a meeting to plot strategy. Little by little, however, the combined efforts of businessmen began to stifle muckraking and reform."[110]

Between 1905 and 1916, seven well-known muckraking magazines folded, and in 1912 conservative business interests had bought three well-known muckraking publications – *McClure's*, the *American*, and *Collier's*. In the case of the failed *Hampton's* magazine, one of the last of the "attacking" publications, railroad interests interfered with the magazine publisher's ability to secure loans from New York banks. The theft of the company's financial ledgers by an accountant exposed to stockholders that owner Benjamin Hampton was struggling because of his inability to get loans. The magazine folded after Hampton could no longer raise cash.[111]

Russell knew of the fight between the railroads and *Hampton's* because he was at the center. The conflict between *Hampton's* and the rail companies began when Russell wrote a series of articles about the railroad owners that documented Russell's belief that "the whole American railroad business was rotten with fraud and lying."[112] He began the series by tracing the history of how the railroad moguls built their lines and made their fortunes.

Many historians credit the railroad industry as the first big business in the United States because it employed thousands of people, and its business was conducted in several different states. The rates set by the railroad owners "affected whether countless shippers made or lost money

---

109   Ibid, p. 193; see also Robert Miraldi, "The Muckrakers are Chased Away," *Muckraking and Objectivity: Journalism's Colliding Traditions* (Westport, Conn.: Greenwood Press, 1990), pp. 23–80; and, Michael D. Marcaccio, "Did a Business Conspiracy End Muckraking?" A Reexamination," *Historian* 47 (November 1984): pp. 58–71.
110   Miraldi, *Pen is Mightier*, p. 193.
111   Ibid, pp. 188–189.
112   Charles Edward Russell, *Stories of the Great Railroads* (Chicago: Charles H. Kerr & Co., 1912), p 62.

in carrying on a business. The ability of the rail lines to determine the economic health of a town or city, their direct impact on the lives of farmers and manufacturers, and their capacity to influence legislatures and courts all made the railroads a significant political issue."[113]

Russell was personally familiar with the impact of the rails. He grew up in an Iowa farming community that relied on the railroads, and was regularly impacted by what Russell's father called the "lawless, arbitrary manipulation of freight rates" to maximize railroad owner profits.[114] Russell's father, Edward, edited the *Davenport Gazette*. In the 1870s, Edward Russell blasted the rails in his editorials, and as a result one rail line refused to ship coal the *Gazette* needed to run its steam-fired printing press. Edward Russell didn't back down, though, writing that the answer to the problems that the railroads presented was competition.

In 1881, Edward Russell traveled to Washington, D.C. to lobby for a canal that would offer a cheaper transportation alternative to area farmers and businesses. The railroads fought federal funding for the canal, and in 1884, when the fight for a final construction appropriation was at its height, and Russell traveled to D.C. to again lobby for funding, "the railroad and corporate interests" had taken over the *Gazette* (which had previously been sold to a lumber dealer in 1882) and fired Edward Russell as editor.[115]

Charles Edward Russell's *Hampton's* series was republished as a book (*Stories of the Great Railroads*, 1912). His original articles appeared in *Hampton's* in 1910 and they detailed all of the shady deals, bribes, rate manipulations, and fraudulent methods used by the railroad tycoons to build their empires. Russell concluded that the rails in private hands were solely for making money and did not serve the public good. When the railroads expanded to the West and achieved a "physical victory" navigating through the Rocky Mountains, Russell called it "a monstrous

---

113   Lewis I. Gould, *America in the Progressive Era, 1890–1914* (Edinburgh, Pearson Education Limited, 2001), p. 3.
114   Miraldi, *Pen is Mightier*, p. 32.
115   Ibid, p. 32.

triumph of greed, fraud and corruption."[116]

In one of his *Hampton's* articles, Russell said the railroads were a "steadily growing evil" that was "more menacing than any problem any nation has ever dealt with." At the time of Russell's railroad articles, *Hampton's* had a circulation of 425,000. The railroad owners had taken notice, and before a November 1910 article was to be published about the rail lines owned by William H. Vanderbilt, a representative from the New York Central Railroad called *Hampton's* and threatened to pull all of the railroad's advertising if Russell's story ran. *Hampton's* ignored the threat, ran the story, and lost the advertising. In another instance that fall, a representative of the New York, New Haven and Hartford Rail Company threatened that "the financial powers" backing the rail company would "ruin the magazine" if a story about that rail line was published. It was soon after this story ran that the New York banks refused to give Benjamin Hampton loans.[117]

Russell wrote of the episode: "Mr. Hampton was ruined according to prediction and his magazine was swept out of his hands." Despite the fact that *Hampton's* had large circulation and strong advertising revenues even without the railroads, "not a bank in New York would advance it one dollar."[118]

The "Controlling Interests," as Russell called them, did manage to strike some meaningful blows to the muckraking magazines, as noted in the case of *Hampton's*. Miraldi suggests that several other factors also likely led to the general decline in muckraking. This included the realization of some of the social reforms that many of the muckraking journalists sought, such as banking reform and food and drug controls, as well as the expansion of the federal government to control some of the "excesses of industrialism."[119]

Declining magazine circulation also suggests the public may have been less interested in journalism that was exposing wrongdoing than it

---

116   Ibid, p. 190.
117   Russell, *Stories of the Great Railroads*, pp. 5–7.
118   Ibid, p. 7.
119   Miraldi, *Pen is Mightier*, p. 194.

had been previously. Historian Richard B. Kielbowicz writes that it was "editors' lack of business acumen, the saturation of the market with too many similar magazines, and a decline in public interest" that were the most likely causes of changes in ownership at many of the muckraking magazines, rather than a grand conspiracy. He notes that as magazines became more "flush with advertising" they generally became more conservative and less progressive after about 1912.[120] Whatever the cause of the decline in the muckraking publications, Russell saw this ultimately as a struggle between the people and big corporate interests. According to Miraldi: "For Russell, the attack on and demise of *Hampton's* was proof that the "people" were in a war with the "interests." And while most of the muckrakers turned to other pursuits, Russell kept fighting the war, becoming, in fact, more obsessed – almost paranoid – about the dangerous might of the capitalists."[121]

---

120   Richard B. Kielbowicz, "Postal Subsidies for the Press and the Business of Mass Culture, 1880–1920," *Business History Review* 64 (Autumn, 1990), pp. 451–488, p. 481.
121   Miraldi, *Pen is Mightier*, p. 194.

Chapter 4

Public Opinion & the Public Lecture Circuit

Despite the decline in muckraking journals between 1908 and 1915, Russell was one of several muckrakers who continued to practice investigatory and exposé journalism. His style during this time was often to include long quotations from documents (such as the letters he excerpts in the 1914 *Pearson's* article featured in this chapter), detailed charts and other dry forms of data, in addition to weaving in anecdotes. While the article republished below continues to build on Russell's concerns about newspaper ownership and outside corporate influences on news reporting, Russell's article also challenges what he called, "One of the greatest engines of public thought in this country," the Chautauqua tent circuit.[122]

Although most people today know little about the Chautauqua tent circuit of the early 20th century, it was very influential both at the time, and in its lasting impact on the structure and operation of the modern-day public lecture circuit, where agents book prominent speakers to share their thoughts with audiences across the country for speaking and transportation fees. Like the Chautauqua circuits a hundred years ago, today's speakers are typically current and former politicians, academics, journalists, public intellectuals, musicians and entertainers.

The Chautauqua tent circuit drew its name from what is now called the Chautauqua Institution in Chautauqua, New York. Originally, a Methodist minister and an inventor/entrepreneur founded Chautauqua (then called the Fair Point Sunday School Assembly) to create an annual Sunday school meeting that would improve religious education among the established Protestant sects.[123] Fair Point held its first assembly in

---

122 Charles Edward Russell, "How Business Controls News," *Pearson's Magazine* (vol. 31, no. 5, May 1914).
123 Theodore Morrison, *Chautauqua: A Center for Education, Religion, and*

Chautauqua in 1874. The success of the first assembly led the founders
to invite a high-profile speaker to kick off the second assembly during
the summer of 1875. When President Ulysses S. Grant spoke to the
crowd of thirty thousand before the second meeting at Chautauqua, word
about the assembly quickly spread. In 1876, Chautauqua's popularity
allowed it to expand its programming to include a "Scientific Congress"
that provided popular education in the physical and biological sciences,
and a "Temperance Convention" that featured Chautauqua's first woman
speaker (a strong supporter of women's suffrage, but she did not speak
on that topic).[124]

In its earliest inception, the tent circuit sought to build on the success
of the Lyceum Movement from the 1830s, and the Chautauqua Literary
and Scientific Circuit (CLSC), an educational program offered by Chautauqua a few years after the first assembly was held. The CLSC began
in 1878 as a program of guided reading. In essence, the CLSC was a
book club. One of the Chautauqua founders, John Vincent, conceived of
the idea early in his thinking about the national Sunday school assembly.

> [He] insisted that education never ended till the grave, that it was
> for all men and women of every kind and station in life. For those
> who did not have the opportunity to undertake college or graduate
> training ... he was convinced that a program of guided reading could
> at least initiate them into the "college outlook," give them a baseline
> from which to advance, and give their children the stimulation of a
> home where knowledge and educational ambition were respected.[125]

At its core, Chautauqua was about education, whether religious,
scientific or literary. As it expanded its programs, one of its primary
goals was to make education available to the masses. This was seen in
Chautauqua's various outreach programs, including the CLSC. The CLSC
alone was so popular that by 1918 it had nearly doubled its enrollment to

---

the Arts in America (Chicago: The University of Chicago Press, 1974).
124   Morrison, pp. 32–33.
125   Ibid, p. 52.

300,000 people across the country.[126]

The Chautauqua tent circuit sought to emulate the goals of the CLSC by bringing to mostly rural and small-town America important speakers to spark debate on important issues of the time. The goal was to expose a wide swath of the citizenry to lectures and debates, much like the CLSC exposed a larger group of the population to literature and important writings, coupled with discussions about what they read.

The basic model for a lecture circuit was already in place. In 1831, the American Lyceum Association was founded to unite a chain of intellectual societies for weekly lectures and debates. According to one account of the association, American philosopher and writer Ralph Waldo Emerson called it "a good pulpit," and many famous thinkers and writers of the time participated.[127] Perhaps the most famous was Mark Twain, but other notable speakers included Elizabeth Cady Stanton, Susan B. Anthony, and William Lloyd Garrison. The Lyceum movement began locally in Boston, but became so popular through the 19th century and into the early 20th century that it reached across the nation. Most of the lectures and subsequent performances were held through the winter. When the Chautauqua lectures began, they filled the gap left during the summer (Chautauqua traditionally ran most of its programs in the summer).[128]

The first Chautauqua tent lecture was in Iowa in 1904; by 1910, tent circuits proliferated rapidly because a plan of operation and a basic structure was established. By 1921, Chautauqua had nearly 100 circuits that reached 9,597 communities in the United States and Canada, and an estimated 40 million people purchased either single or season-ticket admission.[129] Although the Chautauqua name was attached to most of these circuits, not all of them were directly connected to the Chautauqua Institution in New York. According to Chautauqua historian Theodore Morrison, some communities and circuit promoters used the Chautau-

---

126   Ibid.
127   Harry P. Harrison, *Culture Under Canvas: The Story of Tent Chautau-qua* (New York: Hasting House Publishers, 1958).
128   Morrison, p. 181.
129   Ibid.

qua name when in reality they had no affiliation. When the affiliation was legitimate, Chautauqua generally assisted the tent circuits through leadership, staff sharing, and moral support, but not through financial assistance. The Chautauqua circuits each paid their own speakers and according to Morrison they resisted business or other efforts to subsidize lectures.[130]

While it was likely true that the circuits that were legitimately connected to Chautauqua in New York were not formally in partnership with specific businesses, it's likely not the case for many of the other circuits that still used the Chautauqua name but weren't directly affiliated. Harry Harrison, who worked for decades as a Chautauqua circuit manager, wrote in his memoir that the circuits were very profitable. He writes that the man who created the structure for the Chautauqua circuits' success was Keith Vawter, a showman who was responsible for marrying "the respectability of the Lyceum to the spangles of the stage, naming the union 'Chautauqua' after an institution established permanently on Chautauqua Lake, New York." Harrison called this version of the Chautauqua tent circuit "show business."[131]

Whether the tent circuit was an offshoot of the real Chautauqua or simply named in honor of Chautauqua, historians agree the circuits had tremendous impact on public opinion. This is why the questions raised by Russell in the following article are important – did the same corporate interests that influenced much of the news also have influence on the public lecture circuit that captured such large audiences across the country? Very little, if anything, had been written about this at the time. Russell's 1914 article, reprinted in this chapter, is notable for its attempt to expose corporate and political influence within the Chautauqua tent circuits.

According to Harrison, who worked in the circuits, "Inside the big brown tents, millions of Americans first heard impassioned pleas for a

---

130   Morrison, p. 183. Robert Miraldi, Russell's biographer, estimates that the circuits reached 30 million people in about 12,000 towns. See Robert Miraldi, *The Pen is Mightier: The Muckraking Life of Charles Edward Russell* (New York, Palgrave MacMillan, 2003), p. 211.
131   Harrison, p. viii.

Federal income tax, slum clearance, free schoolbooks, world disarmament." Topics included Theodore Roosevelt's New Nationalism of 1912, Woodrow Wilson's New Freedom, Robert LaFollette's National Progressive program, and, according to Harrison, contained a range of political ideas. Some examples offered by Harrison were "tariff revision, the initiative, referendum and recall, woman suffrage, prohibition of child labor, a corrupt practices act, and dozens of other social ideas."[132]

Morrison, however, writes that leading up to World War I,

> The circuits rode the tide of patriotism that the war itself set in motion, when audiences would respond night after night to "Keep the Home Fires Burning." In turn, the circuits did their bit for the war effort. "President Wilson," writes [Charles F.] Horner [who supervised a report for the bureau of statistical research on the International Lyceum and Chautauqua Association] "appreciated the wide and direct channels for information which the platform commanded, and he declared that the Lyceum and Chautauqua were an integral part of the National Defense."[133]

The primary criticism of the circuits at the time was that they were ripe for both public and private pressures to control who spoke and on which topics, because the organizational structure relied on local committees and platform managers. Writer and educator Glenn Frank suggested in a 1919 *Century Magazine* article that the tent circuits should have followed a model like the Ford Hall Forum in Boston, which was founded in 1908 and still exists today as the nation's oldest continuously operating free public lecture series.[134] Frank wrote, "The Lyceum and Chautauqua represent an extensive national machinery of influence, reaching into all sorts of communities. With the exception of the church and the public

---

132   Ibid, pp. 90–96.
133   Morrison, p. 181.
134   Morrison, p. 183. See also Kevin Mattson, *Creating a Democratic Public: The Struggle for Urban Participatory Democracy During the Progressive Era* (State College, Pa.: The Pennsylvania State University Press, 1998) p. 45; and, www.fordhallforum.org.

school, no word-of-mouth institution equals its scope."[135]

Russell and many of his muckraking colleagues knew the Chautauqua circuit well from the inside. Russell, Ida Tarbell, Lincoln Steffens and Will Irwin all were paid to give lectures, and between 1910 and 1912 Russell was a regular performer. In his autobiography, Russell acknowledged that the Chautauquas were meant to blend culture and profit, but that he thought it was "a great educational factor" in raising public consciousness about many important issues. Most of the time, Russell lectured on what he and other socialists called "the unconsumed surplus," which focused on the high levels of poverty in America at a time when the country had great wealth and a surplus of unconsumed goods.[136]

Despite his participation in the Chautauqua circuit and his acknowledgement of its educational value, Russell was not a fan. When radio became popular in the 1920s, Russell applauded it because "it killed the Chautauqua." Although radio and other forms of entertainment helped steer people away from the Chautauqua tent circuits during the 1920s, it wasn't until 1933 that they formally ceased to exist.[137]

•   •   •

How Business Controls News
By Charles Edwards Russell[138]

The fact is, Brethren, for the very existence of this system under which the masses are impoverished and the few are enriched, the control of the public press is the first necessity.

"In this republic," chirrup the trained parrots of platitude, "public opinion rules supreme and no arbitrary power used for private advantage can withstand it."

Sure. Fine. But suppose there is an arbitrary power able to control,

135   Glenn Frank, "The Parliament of the People," *Century Magazine*, July, 1919.
136   Miraldi, p. 212.
137   Miraldi, p. 212; Morrison, p. 184.
138   Russell, "How Business Controls News."

master and direct public opinion. What then?

Then this very public opinion supposed by superficial thinkers to be the safeguard and bulwark of our freedom becomes the exact means by which we are enslaved and the autocrats rule, does it not?

And that is the actual situation today and the real reason why the autocratic power of the Controlling Interests must master and has mastered every means by which public opinion is influenced, suggested and molded. It is the final reason why we have not and cannot have at present a free press.

This power must dominate our periodical literature. If it cannot dominate in one way it will in another. By purchase, by control, by withholding the advertising, by intimidation or by social influence it must control the current literature that you read and on which you base your opinion.

Two or three years ago the old *Boston Traveller*, which had always been a nice old respectable lady in the journalistic sewing circle, was bought by a young man of large independent means and pronounced ideas as to what should be a free and untrammeled press. He looked about for a man of courage and ability to conduct the *Traveller* on lines of absolute accuracy, fairness and legitimate news, and selected Mr. Marlin Pew, who had won the place for an executive in the independent Scripps-McRae Service to which I referred in a previous article.

Mr. Pew had both character and courage and he was an expert newspaper commander. He began at once to make the *Traveller* conspicuous in Boston by printing the news without regard to the Controlling Interests, the advertisers or any other throttling influence. The paper began to gain greatly in circulation, but it also won the bitter hatred of the Interests. Every conceivable effort was made to sway the proprietor and induce him to suppress or dismiss Mr. Pew. All the power of business, social and personal affiliations was brought to bear. Strange to say, all of these failed. They have seldom or never failed before. But this young man was determined to have his way and to see if there could not be published in this country one newspaper free from the gag.

But, unluckily, after a few months the young man died, and soon afterward the fact was disclosed that from his estate the *Traveller* had been bought by the head of the Shoe Machinery Trust.

This Trust has been investigated by the United States Government. It is a great and famous power in New England, and, if you wish to know its reputation for rapacity and ruthlessness, ask any shoe manufacturer or refer to the writings on this subject by Judson C. Welliver.

The head of the Shoe Machinery Trust now summoned Mr. Pew to his presence and endeavored first by commands, then by intimidation, then by cajolery to induce him to put on the soft pedal. Mr. Pew was not impressed. He flashed upon the new owner a contract he had made with the previous proprietor that gave to Mr. Pew absolute and unfettered control of the news and editorial departments and composing room of the *Traveller*. Mr. Pew had a competent notion of existing newspaper conditions, and had drawn this contract so as to make his power unquestionable.

He continued to make of the *Traveller* exactly such a newspaper as he had made before. One day he caught on the ticker a line that indicated to his experienced mind the possible existence of a piece of great and suppressed financial news. He sent forth some of his ablest reporters, and they turned up an astonishing story of legitimate and veritable news affecting one of the largest financial houses in Boston. This story he instructed his reporters to write exactly in accordance with the facts.

They had scarcely begun to put pencil to paper before another brokerage house called him on the phone, told him they understood his reporters had been making inquiries about this story and informed him that he must not print it. Mr. Pew replied that the story would be in the afternoon's edition and rang off.

In a few moments a leading and influential legal firm, one of the most famous and influential firms in Boston, rang up, told him they had been informed he intended to publish this story, and that on no account must it be printed, as it would seriously affect important business interests. Mr. Pew replied that the story would be in the afternoon's edition and rang off.

Five minutes later the door opened and in bounced the business manager of the *Traveller*, greatly excited. He said:

"You're not going to print that story about the Blank firm, are you?"

"I am," said Mr. Pew, "this afternoon."

"But, my dear man," said the business manager, "don't you understand that the most important business interests in Boston will be antagonized by the printing of that story?"

"That is not my affair," said Mr. Pew. "The story is legitimate news, it is perfectly true, and it goes into this afternoon's edition."

By this time the copy for the story was on its way to the composing room. In ten minutes the business manager returned, still more excited. He said:

"You absolutely must not print that story."

"Look here!" said Mr. Pew. "By my contract I have sole control of the editorial department and the composing room. You have nothing to say about them. That story is going into type and the type is going into the forms. You can stop the presses if you wish, but if you print the paper at all you'll print it with that story in it. Is that clear? And another thing. Somebody sent you here to try to stop that story. Who was it?"

"Well," said the business manager, "it was the big boss himself," meaning the head of the Shoe Machinery trust.

"I thought so," said Mr. Pew. "You tell him that if he can break my contract in any way he can keep that story out, otherwise it will go in."

The manager disappeared and was back in five minutes.

"We'll buy your contract," said he.

"You'll have to buy it from this minute to the utmost extent of its term," said Mr. Pew.

The business manager produced his check book.

"No check," said Mr. Pew. "I know too much to take checks. Cash or nothing."

"I can't get the cash at this hour of day," said the manager, "and you know a check is just as good."

"Cash or nothing," said Mr. Pew.

The business manager was back again in fifteen minutes with his hands full of bills. On the spot he paid the entire amount called for by Mr. Pew's contract, which stipulated a large salary and had years yet to run.

Mr. Pew closed his desk and went out of the office and the type of the story was snatched out of the form in the composing room just in time to prevent the publicity to which the Interests objected.

If they do not win in one way they win in another, always they win.

In Indianapolis the Controlling Interests are expressed in a combination of the street railroad company and other public utilities, the great retail business houses and the banks. About a dozen years ago the capitalization of the street railroad company was increased by a series of manipulations from $3,250,000 to $57,000,000. To provide additional business for firms that assisted or connived at these manipulations the street railroad company brought every car from all its routes down to a loop of two blocks in the heart of the city where these business houses were located, so that every passenger, willy-nilly, must be carried in front of them. The same all powerful combination embraced the water company and the telephone company and was preparing similar exploits in financing with these utilities.

The employees of the street railroad had never been organized. In August, 1913, an effort was made to form a union among these men. The street railroad company for sufficient reasons was opposed to labor organizations. Similarly, of course, all the other components of the Controlling Interests were opposed to such organization. Similarly, therefore, all the influences swayed by the Controlling Interests were opposed to such organization. For in Indianapolis as elsewhere the merchants existed under the fists of the banks and the newspapers under the fists of the merchants, and the city government under the fists of all these and whatever the Interests wanted they got and in short order.

In this instance these fists put the kibosh on every newspaper in Indianapolis except one. Only one newspaper mentioned the fact that the street-car men were trying to organize or told how the company sought to prevent organization. Some of these efforts on the company's part, by the way, made pretty fair news. What would you say, for instance, to a crowd of automobiles so stationed outside the hall where the men were to meet that all their headlights fell upon the entrance and the company's spotters took down the name of every man that went in? What would you think of gangs of imported gunmen that shot or beat up the men favoring the union and all but killed a reporter that ventured upon the scene?

Fairly interesting news – what?

But only one newspaper, the Indianapolis *Sun*, reported these things. The *Sun* had lately changed hands. Its new proprietorship had no interest in labor organizations and at that time little enlightenment as to fundamental social conditions. But it thought news was news and had to be printed, so it reported the beatings, maulings and shootings by the thugs of the street railroad company as it would have reported similar outrages by anybody else.

Thereupon the head of a firm that is one of the heaviest advertisers in Indianapolis, a great and well-known department store, sent for the editor of the *Sun* and kindly but firmly told him to cut out all that labor stuff and cease to interfere with public utility corporations that had at heart the best interests of the community.

To this the editor of the *Sun* responded courteously that the news policy of the paper could not be influenced by any considerations of business. The *Sun* had for sale certain advertising space. Whosoever bought it bought it with no control over the *Sun's* opinions or news columns.

Whereupon that department store cut down its advertising in the *Sun* and was followed therein by most of the other advertisers of the city that were members of the Merchants' Association. They have a Merchants' Association in Indianapolis. Personally, I have not known a city where such stunts as I am about to relate could be pulled off that did not have its Merchants' Association, nor a Merchants' Association that was not the ready, efficient and smoothly working tool of the Controlling Interests to throttle free speech, crush labor organizations and maintain the sanctity of things as they are. Merchants' Associations are always highly respectable. Some of them are so respectable that by comparison they make vice almost decent.

The advertisers that were members of the Indianapolis Merchants' Association kept carefully under the lee of the law. They did not in a body withdraw all their advertising from the *Sun*; to do so might bring down indictments for conspiracy. The conspiracy laws never have been enforced against respectable members of a Merchants' Association; only against low, common members of a labor union. But still they might be enforced equally against both. You never can tell.

Some day some vile demagogue might try to enforce the laws against the rich as much as against the poor. Therefore, play safely by cutting a page advertisement to an inch. That's the game everywhere, and it is good. Applies the garrote in good shape and involves nobody. What's the use of leaving tell-tale tracks around when they're unnecessary?

On November 1st the street-car men struck. The *Sun* took neither side in the controversy. It had no particular sympathy with the men; it stood merely for fair play and to print all the news in sight. On November 4th, the strike continuing and the public inconvenience being great, the *Sun*, in an editorial, urged arbitration. The people took up the suggestion, a huge public meeting endorsed it, clergymen reiterated it, and the company was forced to yield. It had in the beginning announced, as such companies commonly announce, that it had nothing to arbitrate. On this point it was now driven to surrender.

The strike had caused the Chamber of Commerce to form a so-called "Safety Committee," whose real function seems to have been to safeguard the watered capitalization of the street railroad company. A week after the men had returned to their work pending arbitration this "Safety Committee" summoned before it representatives of all the Indianapolis newspapers and told them that the street railroad employees had broken the settlement contract and that therefore more trouble was at hand. How had the contract been broken? Why, the men had insisted upon recognition of their union. But the terms of the agreement expressly bound both sides to try first to settle any difference by conciliation and, this failing, to leave it to arbitration. The men had not refused to arbitrate their demand about the recognition of their union. Until they should so refuse no one could say they had broken their contract and no just cause could arise for renewing the strife.

As a matter of face, of course, the company merely wished to evade the agreement it had made, and, being better prepared now for a struggle, intended to crush the union.

The committee proceeded to give to the newspaper representatives explicit instructions as to the course their journals were to pursue in the new emergency; what should and what should not be printed.

The *Sun* declared that it would heed no such instructions, and that so long as the men were willing to arbitrate their grievances they had not broken the agreement. The editor of the *Sun* said so in plain terms in print.

This stopped the company's move. But just at that time a fresh scare was started among the employers by a report that the teamsters of the city were organizing and about to strike. Should they strike, business, it was said, would be paralyzed.

At this, in a kind of panic, a Vehicle Protective Association was formed to fight the threatened strike. Shanks, the Mayor, whose efforts to lower the cost of living with a public market system made him famous, was forced to resign by the Controlling Interests because they did not believe he would use the city government against the strikers. The Vehicle Protective Association then requested the Merchants' Association to withdraw all advertising from any newspaper that should print any detailed report of a teamsters' strike, should one occur, or to display sympathy on the side of labor.

It then imported about three hundred gun-men and gangsters and held them in readiness.

On November 30th the teamsters struck and the gangsters, assisted by the city police, began their operations.

In flagrant violation of two state statutes the imported ruffians had been sworn in as special police.

For the most part they were mounted; all were heavily armed. Their function was to charge upon citizens, beating and shooting, that they might create such a reign of terror that public opinion would force an ending of the strike.

In these operations they killed four persons. One was a colored elevator boy. He was walking along the street to his work and was shot down by gun-men from a wagon half a block away.

None of the perpetrators of these murders was prosecuted.

The *Sun* reported these things and protested against them.

Then the merchants called an indignation meeting against the *Sun*, denounced it and demanded a rigid boycott of its advertising columns.

Immediately all the local business advertisements dropped out of the *Sun*.

It is now maintaining its fight against these odds. The plain people of Indianapolis have shown their sympathy with its brave struggle by increasing its circulation from 17,000 to 40,000, the largest in the city, but the Controlling Interests have decreed its destruction and the plain people have little advertising to dispense.

Under such conditions, no wonder the average newspaper is very careful to be "good" and do as it is told. It is manufactured at a loss. The sales price covers only a part of the manufacturing cost. Therefore, to live it must have much advertising. The advertising it must have is in the hands of business men dominated by the banks and the banks are dominated by the Controlling Interests. What was plainly declared in the case of the Indianapolis *Sun* is conveyed frankly or covertly to newspapers everywhere.

If they print what is objectionable to the Controlling Interests they cannot get the advertising they must have to live.

It is a strangle hold. Nothing can escape it.

Therefore the news columns are poisoned and perverted. Therefore news is suppressed or distorted. Therefore we have no such thing as a free press in America, but a censorship as active and effective as any in Russia or Spain.

When you read any item in your newspaper, no matter how innocent it may seem, however veritable or well founded, you never know how insidiously it may have been doped, doctored, or twisted to create in your mind a certain impression useful to the Controlling Interests and inimical to you.

I will give one illustration.

The Controlling Interests very much desired to secure the repeal of the exemption of American coastwise ships from the Panama Canal tolls. They desired this for more than one reason, but chiefly because they owned the Trans-continental Railroads and wished to cripple the competition of the canal.

To bring about the repeal they created through their newspapers the belief that the United States is bound by treaty obligations not to discriminate in favor of American ships in the canal.

There is no such obligation; everyone who has carefully considered the Hay-Pauncefote Treaty knows we are bound in no such way. But by continually asserting the obligation and referring to it as an admitted thing the kept newspapers of the Interests have succeeded in putting over this monstrous fake and inducing the country to believe in it.

Who will assert now that there is any real government in this country except the government of the – Controlling Interests?

But let us see more of the workings of this colossal power of newspaper censorship as exercised by the Interests.

At Akron, Ohio, the chief industry is the making of rubber tires. The tire companies are wealthy and powerful. They dominate the banks; the banks dominate the merchants; the merchants dominate the expressions of public opinion. It is a familiar situation and perfectly typical. Every other city with a big industry presents the like of it.

The workers in the tire factories were badly treated and badly paid. Their work is unhealthful and arduous. About a year ago they struck for better conditions.

The Akron *Press*, the principal newspaper of the town, supported the cause of the strikers.

The tire companies pulled the strings on the banks and the banks pulled the strings on the merchants. That was all. The merchants were warned not to advertise in the *Press*; any merchant that disregarded the warning found that his bank would not carry him when he needed the accommodations. That did the trick. To the average merchant banking accommodations are the arterial blood supply to business. You might as well cut a merchant's jugular as shut off his banking accommodations.

So the merchants joined the boycott of the *Press*. Many of them hated to do it, for it is a popular journal, but nothing else was possible. The advertisements went out of the *Press*. Its circulation rose and continues to rise. People at large like its courage and independence; therefore they buy it. But the local merchants will not advertise in it. They do not care – with the club of the banks held over their heads.

Cincinnati offers another illustration and the best, because it shows the ramifications of this power.

Cincinnati had for many years about the worst municipal government in America. I know this seems to be saying much, when we think of Philadelphia, Pittsburgh, Buffalo, St. Louis, San Francisco and other claimants in the old days to the bad eminence in city misrule that has made us a byword around the world. Nevertheless in any such comparison I am strong for Cincinnati. Considering its size I don't see how any other community could have done worse. When the Cox gang was supreme Cincinnati was municipally so rotten the very name stunk, and in ten years the city made little growth in population. People fled from a place so rankly misgoverned.

As usual in such conditions the highest circles of finance and society went hand in hand with the men that at every election deposited 15,000 fraudulent votes, ruled the city, rioted in corruption and organized and commercialized vice. The gang gave to the respectable element corporation franchises and privileges that conferred almost illimitable power; the respectable element gave to the gang its cordial but concealed support, meanwhile praising God in public places while pilfering of the poor.

In Cincinnati, also, the public utility Interests were closely knit; likewise the financiers and the merchants. So far it was the invariable condition. But in Cincinnati the control of the press extended to the point where, with one exception, the papers commonly stood for the corrupt gang, which is going pretty far, and farther than usual. It shows again the truly appalling power swayed by these Interests. Some of the newspapers were controlled by the most eminent and immaculate gentlemen in the city's business and social life. These were also interested in public utility enterprises and such enterprises flourished through the aid of the gang. This connection was largely the key of the situation.

The one newspaper that would not tolerate the gang was the Cincinnati *Post*. For ten years it waged ceaseless war upon the corrupt machine. At last it won, drove out the gang and sent the head thereof to permanent retirement.

Also the *Post* earned the enduring hatred of the Controlling Interests by fighting the various manipulations of the public utilities. The gas company and the electric lighting company had been virtually consolidated, through a great holding company that took and concealed the tribute gathered from a patient public. The *Post* slammed into this arrangement.

A law of the state of Ohio forbad corporation franchises of a longer term than twenty-five years. In the course of the high finance of the Interests that owned the Cincinnati traction system a longer term became very desirable for profits. So a bill was quietly rushed through the Ohio legislature to enable city councils to grant franchises up to fifty years. Instantly the city council of Cincinnati, gang-ruled, put through an ordinance extending the franchise of the Cincinnati Traction Company to fifty years. The *Post* and other free journals in Ohio savagely attacked the new law and the manner of its passing, so that in a few days the frightened legislature made haste to undo its work, but the Cincinnati ordinance still stood.

After a time a moral revulsion swept over misgoverned Ohio and a new style of lawmaker coming in the *Post* began an earnest campaign to secure a repeal of the Cincinnati traction company's extension.

"That will be about all," said the disgusted Interests when they felt the force of this campaign. A strike of street-car men in Cincinnati followed by a strike of teamsters as in Indianapolis, gave the desired opportunity. In both instances the *Post* was fair and just to the men. The Interested pulled the string on the banks, the banks pulled the string on the merchants. Down came the boycott in full swing. The merchants pulled out their advertising. The *Post* had the largest circulation in the city; its circulation is much larger now than when the strike began, for people admire its attempts to be independent. But the merchants do not dare to advertise in it.

In Los Angeles the *Record*, because it defended the labor unions when the story of the MacNamaras was a current issue, and was regarded as a labor champion, has borne for nearly three years the full weight of a similar boycott. Of course in Los Angeles the spirit of the Controlling Interests is most perfectly typified in General Otis, whose sweet and genial reasonableness on the subject of labor is well known. Neither department stores nor the humblest merchant in Los Angeles would dare to advertise in the *Record* until the Controlling Interests may be pleased to lift the ban. Instances have been collected of small business men, who, on account of the *Record's* large circulation would like to advertise in it, but under the threat of the banks, do not dare to so much as express their opinion about it except in whispers to confidential friends.

The warfare that has been made on the San Francisco *Bulletin*, for the like reasons and by the same influences, was discussed in a previous article. But in San Francisco labor is both well organized and alert. It understands that the *Bulletin* is being penalized for telling the truth about existing conditions and for being sympathetic with labor and labor therefore is rallying to the *Bulletin's* support. This indicates a potent remedy for our press censorship. If we and our families refuse to purchase of merchants that boycott a truth-telling newspaper we can effectively weaken the censorship.

In a certain western town the department stores wished to have an old cemetery turned into building lots that more customers might be housed convenient to the stores. They compelled all the newspapers except one to advocate the obliteration of the cemetery and then boycotted the newspaper that stood out. A circle of women was sentimentally opposed to the destruction of the old cemetery and sympathized with the newspaper that refused to do the department store's will.

One woman went to the principal store and withdrew her account, giving as a reason the attitude of this store toward the rebellious newspaper. Within an hour the frightened proprietor had renewed his advertisement in that newspaper and the boycott was broken.

While all men of any observation know fairly well the outline of the facts about newspaper censorship, nearly all cherish the belief that the public platform remains a free and untrammeled vehicle of opinion. If a man is not allowed to write the truth in magazines and newspapers he can at least say what he pleases on the stump. It will astonish all persons that have clung to this belief to know that the Controlling Interests have been busy with the lecture platform also.

One of the greatest engines of public thought in this country is the

Chautauqua of which many hundreds are held in this country every year. In most places the Chautauqua is directed by the local bankers and merchants. In recent years there has developed a special brand of eloquence for use at these assemblies known as "Chautauqua Optimism." It glorifies the greatness of America, assures us that all is perfectly lovely with us and piously slams the muckrakers. Among the favorite dispensers of this style of oratory are the Honorable Charles B. Landis[139] and the Honorable James E. Watson.[140] I was reading not long ago some press-agent eulogies on Mr. Watson's work on these lines, and it seemed to be perfectly grand. It appeared that Mr. Watson viewed all muckrakers and other disturbers of our social harmony with extreme disapproval and his discourses could be warranted to produce a soothing effect in any community.

We have now the advantage of some documentary evidence showing the true origin of this pleasant line of dope.

Before the United States Senate Committee investigating the Mulhall revelations and the National Association of Manufacturers; examination of the Honorable Charles B. Landis:

> Mr. Landis (in answer to a question): I delivered a lecture on the title "The Message of an Optimist." It was a cheerful message that I delivered to the people of Missouri and Iowa, and I think probably Minnesota and other states in the West.

It appeared that Mr. Landis had another lecture for Chautauqua listeners on the subject of the "American Merchant Marine."

> Question by Senator Reed: Who were "We"?
> Mr. Landis Well, I was one of the "We."
> Senator Reed: Who was the other "We"?
> Mr. Landis: The Merchant Marine League of Cleveland Ohio.
> Senator Reed: And you were in their pay that summer, were you not?

---

139 Charles Landis was a U.S. Representative from Indiana.
140 James Watson was a U.S. Representative and a U.S. Senator from Indiana.

Mr. Landis: Yes. They paid me, but they did not pay me very much money.

Senator Reed: That was generally known as the ship subsidy lobby, was it not?

Mr. Landis: No, sir, I think not. The whole thing was over at that time as far as legislation went, but they desired very much that some one should talk along that line before the chautauquas of the West.

Senator Reed: And you went out?

Mr. Landis: And I went out, and that was one of the themes on which I talked.

Senator Reed: Did you get pay from the chautauquas as well as from the ship subsidy people?

Mr. Landis: Yes, I did.

A little further along:

Mr. Landis: My recollection now is that my compensation and expenses were paid jointly between the Chautauqua people and the Merchant Marine League of Cleveland, Ohio.

Senator Reed: What Chautauqua circuit did you follow that year?

Mr. Landis: It was the Redpath-Vawter Circuit.[141]

This luminous revelation of the Controlling Interests at work upon the Chautauqua circuits will add great zest, no doubt, to the perusal of the extraordinary correspondence that follows. From these letters it might be deemed that the fountain of Mr. Watson's eloquent optimism would not run dry nor the soothing influence of the Chautauqua cease to radiate through a thousand communities so long as the National Association of Manufacturers had a dollar and the Chautauqua orators a hand that

---

141   The Redpath-Vawter Chautauqua circuit booked events west of the Mississippi River and was named after James Redpath and Keith Vawter. Redpath organized the most famous lectures on the Lyceum movement circuit immediately following the Civil War and ran the Boston Lyceum bureau. Vawter, as noted earlier, was the genius behind marrying the Lyceum with entertainment and naming it after Chautauqua. The Redpath-Vawter circuit was independent of the tent circuits affiliated with Chautauqua, New York, and was highly profitable.

could be raised in glorification of existing conditions.

The letters signed "Secretary" are from Mr. Ferdinand C. Schwedtman. He was secretary of the National Council for Industrial Defense, which was the inner circle of the National Association of Manufacturers and arranged the maneuvers.

September 13, 1909.

Mr. A. E. PALMER
Central Lyceum Bureau,
Kansas City, Mo.

My Dear Mr. Palmer:

I have just returned from a conference of the officers of the National Council for Industrial Defense in New York, and I find your two letters of the 8th and 10th. I will take up the two propositions covered therein in separate letters, but I want to speak here of our Chautauqua program.

The plans outlined to you during your recent visit to Saint Louis were thoroughly approved by the officers of the Council, and I am under instructions from the chairman to arrange for two speakers as quickly as possible. One of these is Mr. Emory, about whom I talked to you at great length during your visit . . . Remember that our idea is to place Mr. Emory on ten or fifteen Chautauqua programs. We want to use every effort to place him on the more prominent parts of the program, and not among a lot of vaudeville actors or negro comedians. . . . He must be placed on the financial basis of high-grade men. You are the best judge of how this can be brought about, as long as you understand that we will absorb Mr. Emory's compensation, and let you and the lyceum managers divide this among you. . . .

The first thing to be arranged now, it seems to me, is Mr. Emory's appearance before the Fork and Knife Club of Kansas City. We send him there entirely at our expense. . . .

Regarding the second or third lecturer, which we may put on next season, I shall write to you in a day or two. It is very likely the man mentioned to you, but I have no authority to use his name so far. I may take a run over to see him to settle all details. . . .

Very truly yours,
Secretary.

.   .   .

This letter was from Schwedtman.

.   .   .

September 29, 1909.

My Dear Sir:

I must make early report regarding our next year's Chautauqua program. If it is absolutely impossible for you to come to St. Louis to discuss the Watson engagement with me I will come to Chicago. The matter must be definitely settled before October 15.

We want Mr. Watson above all others for our educational work, and still this will be only the beginning and we will very likely increase our educational program and our list of speakers very materially within the next twelve months.

You can see the need of getting together because much valuable time has been lost now. Please let us hear from you.

Very truly yours,
Secretary.

Mr. Charles W. Ferguson,
    Chautauqua Managers' Ass'n, Chicago, Ill.

.   .   .

September 29, 1909.

My Dear Friend Watson:

Thank you for your note of September 27th. I have had no further advice from Mr. Ferguson . . . if I cannot get a definite proposition from him soon I recommend that we meet and fix it up. I want to make a report of progress in my Chautauqua mission at an early date, and on October 15th, when some of us meet again in New York, I want to have this definitely out of the way.

You will see from the attached that I have written Mr. Ferguson to-day. I want you above all others to start the ball rolling in our Chautauqua platform educational campaign. Our friend, Emory, will also fill some Chautauqua engagements next summer, and I want to talk over with you one or two prominent men whom we contemplate adding to our list of speakers; your advice on matters of this kind is so much better than that of anybody else. . . .

I note what you say about reaching Mac-Veigh.
With best personal wishes, believe me,
Very truly yours,
Secretary.

Hon. James E. Watson, Rushville, Indiana.

.   .   .

Extract from a long letter from Secretary Schwedtman to J. W. Van Cleave, St. Louis, November 20, 1909:

.   .   .

"Chautauqua Program."

In our various conferences Mr. Kirby and Mr. Emory agreed that
I take upon myself the program of getting a number of Chautauqua
lecturers for next season. I have kept you and them fairly well posted
as to the progress of the work. Definite arrangements have been made
for Watson at a cost of $40 to the Council for every lecture which he
makes to Chautauquas or to organizations on subjects approved by
us. Ex-Congressman Landis, who is a great Chautauqua speaker, is
ready to get in on a similar basis. Mr. Emory has been placed at the
disposal of Chautauqua managers, and they are trying to arrange
dates for him.

You were present when I had a conference with Mr. Ferguson, the
manager of one of the lyceum bureaus I am dealing with, and I think
you were as much impressed as I was with the plans then discussed
of breaking in a number of younger lyceum speakers for our work
without their knowledge and without the knowledge of the public. I
am keeping Ferguson and Palmer and Wagner, the three lyceum men
I am dealing with stirred up, but at best it seems hard work to keep
them moving as fast as we would like to have them move. I would be
very glad to have any suggestions that may come out of a discussion of
this matter with Mr. Kirby or Mr. Emory. Incidentally the preparation
of younger speakers for the platform is going to take a great deal of
somebody's time. Mr. Ferguson would like to have outlined for him
the important points on the various subjects which we want driven
home. It will take days and weeks of study, writing and conferences
to get this well started.

Chicago, Ill., Dec. 8, 1909.

Mr. Fred. C. Schwedtman,
Chemical Building, St. Louis, Mo.

Dear Mr. Schwedtman:

Mr. Charles B. Landis, of Indiana, just called, and I had a very satisfactory talk with him in regard to lecturing on our list in accordance with the suggestions of Mr. Watson.

The Chautauqua business for next summer is perhaps three-fourths booked, but I believe we can get quite a few dates for Mr. Landis yet. I think Mr. Landis is sound and all right. He has had an abundance of experience in Chautauqua work. His Grosvenor debates were popular, and his work was first class. I shall be pleased to take him on, on the same basis as Mr. Watson, if agreeable to you, and if we make this arrangement, I will get after the work immediately, and see if we cannot get a fairly good list of engagements for next summer. I had quite a long talk with Mr. Landis, and he is sound.

There is some competition among the Bureaus for the best of our talent, and I would be glad to have you write me if there are any new developments touching the educational campaign, which you are interested in. As I wrote you a few days ago, there are a number of our younger men, who could fill a good many engagements, and who are sound politically and economically, and who could write good, strong, effective stuff, and who can be handled nicely on this proposition. I would like to improve the opportunities as they go by in landing some of these men, if matters have proceeded far enough, so that you can give me the authority to act. Before any expense is incurred, we might even go so far as to submit the subject matter in manuscript for your inspection.

I shall be very glad to hear from you, and have you send me any literature that is going out, and I will handle this matter personally, and, as we talked, qualifying as best I can for the work.

Yours very truly,

The Chicago Mutual Lyceum Bureau.
Charles W. Ferguson, President.

.   .   .

For the existence of the present system by which the masses are impoverished and the few are enriched the control of the engines of public
thought is indispensable. This is the way the control is absolutely assured
in the news columns of daily journals, in the magazines, on the lecture
platform.

What's the answer?

Chapter 5

Advertising Campaigns and National Consumer Culture

As noted in chapter three, Charles Edward Russell and other journalists of the early 20th century lamented the influence advertising had on newspaper content, often by citing specific examples of direct interference with reporters, editors, articles, and editorials connected to specific issues that challenged advertiser interests. This chapter explores the impact of advertising in a different way. The two articles republished here echo some of the concerns that Russell raised in "The Keeping of the Kept Press," and "How Business Controls the News," but they also offer some additional insights on the impact advertising was beginning to have broadly and on a national scale – in terms of national, coordinated issue-based campaigns, and in terms of a publication's view of its primary purpose. Was it to serve the public and democracy? Or, was it to attract subscribers as potential consumers to continue to build advertising revenue?

The first column offers some reinforcement of the idea that between about 1890 and 1920, "publishers came to regard subscribers less as readers than as consumers to be delivered to merchandisers."[142] Historian Thomas Leonard writes that as the 1920s began, "many journalists conceptualized stories as 'written bait,' to make the public take in ads." E.W. Scripps, one of the men that Russell applauded for his resistance to the growing advertising culture within the news business, was one of the few publishers of the time who would not accept national advertising campaigns, and who instructed his editors to not solicit ads. But, he was

142   Richard B. Kielbowicz, "Postal Subsidies for the Press and the Business of Mass Culture, 1880–1920," *Business History Review* 64 (Autumn, 1990), pp. 451–488, p. 458.

one of the few.[143]

As Robert L. Duffus writes about the continuing conflict between the powerful meat-packing corporations and workers in Chicago, he puts forth an argument that suggests the power of advertising had become so great that specific threats to individual editors were no longer needed. The power of advertising as the primary income source for the press was sufficient enough to reduce editorial page criticisms of positions held by advertisers. And now, these positions played out in well-coordinated, sophisticated national campaigns. How could the editorial pages and columns compete? Would editors even try?

Duffus' article was written several years after passage of the Newspaper Publicity Act in 1912, which was a rider to the 1912 postal appropriations bill passed by Congress. The Newspaper Publicity Act allowed newspapers and magazines to maintain their second-class postage rate (which saved them substantial amounts of money), but only if they disclosed three pieces of financial information to the public – the names of owners and stockholders, published at least twice a year; sworn statements by daily newspapers that asserted accurate circulation figures; and, that all advertising be labeled as such, to avoid confusion between news and advertisements. The last two provisions show the concern that people had about the growing influence of advertising within the press. Many historians have documented that newspapers used vastly inflated circulation numbers to attract advertisers, and that newspapers during this time engaged in "the widespread practice of disguising advertising as news stories and editorials."[144]

.   .   .

---

143   Thomas Leonard, *News for All* (New York: Oxford University Press, 1995), p. 164; See also Daniel Pope, *The Making of Modern Advertising* (New York: Basic Books, 1983), p. 30.
144   Kielbowicz, p. 482.

The Packers and the Press
By Robert L. Duffus

A foot-note to a discussion of the relations between newspapers and advertisers might perhaps be written upon material furnished by the advertising campaign recently entered into by one of the great Chicago packing houses. Every person in the United States who reads at all is probably familiar by this time with the arguments on prices and profit with which this corporation has attempted to refute the damaging testimony given in the hearings of the Federal Trade Commission at Chicago and now embodied in the Commission's report. The validity of this testimony and the integrity of the packers are points which have no bearing upon this aspect of the situation. If ours is a government by public opinion, as we suppose it to be, we are entitled to ask, not only which disputant is the nearer right, but whether each has had a fair hearing before the public. It is at least doubtful if the fundamental requisite of a fair hearing has been met. The side of the packers has been ably presented in a series of advertisements which were frankly partisan. The side of the government has not been so presented. It has been given to the public only in the form of press dispatches, the writers of which were in duty bound not to take a partisan view. The editorial columns of the newspapers have failed almost wholly to exercise that function which is theoretically their sole reason for existence. The cases of the workingmen in the stockyards, of the stock raisers, of the independent slaughter houses, and of the consumers have not been adequately presented by the newspapers.

Every working newspaper man and every one who has thought at all about the supposed and actual functions of newspapers understands what happened and why it happened. On the day after the Trade Commission's hearings had reached their climax an identical advertisement appeared in all the leading papers of Chicago, Kansas City, St. Louis, Omaha, and other cities where the packing industry is of importance. This advertisement was a tribute to the services of the packing corporations and its employees in the war. It contained no reference to the testimony that had been given in Chicago. Within a few weeks, however, advertisements of the same size and general make-up, showing unmistakable signs of being the product of a well-planned campaign, began to appear in the papers of remoter cities and finally in the magazines, and these contained well-written arguments intended to convince the public that the packing houses were not overcharging the consumer or underpaying the producer and were not making excessive profits. They were such arguments as might be presented to a jury by an attorney who had convinced himself of the justice of his case. They were not, and could not be, complete explanations of the meat-packing system. Giving the rate of profit per pound and per year they did not really satisfy the critical mind that the present system of meat-packing was not wasteful and that it did not injure consumer and stock-raiser alike. They did not meet the objections which would have been raised to them had the argument been presented to a jury, and the audience which listened to them did not have the opportunity to listen to an opposing argument or to fearless criticism.

The correctness of this summary few students of newspaper editorials are likely to deny. The newspapers plainly have not discussed the meat situation with anything like the frankness which they would (and do) discuss the nomination of a Non-Partisan League Congressman, despite the fact that meat is felt to be of more pressing and general importance than even several Congressmen. Their failure was not necessarily, or probably, corrupt. The advertising campaign cannot fairly be represented as a bribe. But the relations of newspapers and advertisers are essentially those of customers and patrons, and as in all such relations the traditions of a kind of good will overlapping the terms of the actual contract has grown up. A given newspaper would be of no value to an advertiser if it printed in its editorial column a refutation of claims advanced in the advertising columns; if, for example, it pointed out editorially that the sale of a certain breakfast food in packages was economically wasteful, or that the sales of automobiles should be limited, tough taking pay for advertisements implying the contrary. Besides printing the advertisements the newspaper publisher tacitly agrees not to diminish their effectiveness, and newspaper publishers who do not live up to the terms of this tacit requirement cannot make the newspaper business pay. It is a long step from not attacking advertised goods to not attacking the economic views of the advertiser, yet it is notorious that many newspaper publishers have taken it, and that the test of survival in newspaper publishers is sometimes to be willing to take it.

The case of the investigated packers and their advertising campaign does not lie at the extreme. The packers have given advertisements to newspapers with whose views they cannot possibly agree. The tacit requirement has been merely that the newspapers in question shall not print in their editorial columns refutations of the arguments advanced in their advertising columns. It is not intended to say or hint that the packers themselves would have withdrawn their advertisements from newspapers whose editorial contents nullified them. It is quite possible that their confidence in the greater readability of advertisements as compared with editorials would have led them to overlook such a delinquency. No fact about modern journalism could be more notorious than that the advertisement, as a means of communication between man and man, is at least a generation ahead of the editorial. In a newspaper of a hundred thousand circulation the packers' argument might have reached fifty thousand readers, whereas the editorial refutation could not have hoped under ordinary circumstances to influence more than twenty-five thousand.

But whether the menace of a withdrawal of patronage was real or imaginary it is undeniable that it is always seriously considered by all newspaper publishers, and there is no reason to believe that it was not seriously considered in this instance. The experienced newspaper man knows as well as though he had stood at the elbows of countless editorial writers that the sight of the advertisement automatically checked the impulse to write a frank article about the meat-packing situation. Those who are less completely disillusioned may search the files in vain for a balanced consideration of the case against the packers, although from the news dispatches the public is informed that such a case exists. To use again the simile of legal procedure, the situation is as though a prisoner had been duly indicted and brought into court and the trial conducted with an attorney for the defense but none for the prosecution.

As a war-time government is not dependent directly upon a popular mandate in dealing with such a problem as that now presented in the meat-packing industry no practical harm may be done by the journalistic failure to give it free discussion. Yet every such failure of government by public opinion is a failure of democracy, whatever the practical outcome. The advertisement of propaganda, whether political, personal or economic, is yet in its infancy. We are likely to see, not only political parties, not only armor-plate monopolies and packing-house corporations, but enterprises of more insidious intention, resorting to this weapon increasingly as time goes by. Originally a plain enumeration of goods for sale, the advertisement may become a delicate psychological weapon for undermining popular government by distorting public opinion. The effects of reiteration have been magnificently shown in the sale of dollar watches, safety razors and soap, but the advertisements which produced these sales have been mere kindergarten games, mere playing with letter blocks, compared with those which the application of subtle pens to a close knowledge of popular psychology might produce, provided that newspaper publishers continue to be prevented, by the very laws of their being, from exposing the fallacies, either of advertised hair tonics or advertised ideas. The movement to clean up the advertising columns has gone far, and will go further, but without a revolution in the economic position of the publisher it cannot go far enough to keep the flow of information and argument uncontaminated. We need to have a care lest the very issues of war and peace, of national life or death, of the soul as well as the stomach, be perverted.

.   .   .

The Press & the Post Office

The following editorial from *The Public* is interesting because while it echoes much of what has already been noted about the general corrupting influence of advertising and newspaper consolidation on newspaper content, it also takes a stand against a newly enacted postal zoning provsion that reformed postal policy governing periodicals and newspapers.

The Public fit a category of publication in the teens that magazine historian Theodore Peterson called "journals of opinion, comment, and controversy." He writes that these journals

> walked a lonely and precarious road ... – lonely because their views were invariably the unpopular views of the minority, precarious because they were chronically in financial distress. The mass-produced magazines tended to be neutral or conservative in treating social issues, public affairs, and business once the era of muckraking had ended. ... [The journals of opinion] were often far ahead of their times in their advocacy of social justice and political reform, yet they were an effective instrument for transmuting the ideas of an aggressive minority into those of an inert majority. The influence of the journals of opinion could not be measured by their circulation figures. They directed their messages to the well educated, to the intellectuals, on the premise that in the long run these persons were most influential in determining the course of events.[145]

It was likely financial strain coupled with the strong desire to share its opinions with a national audience that led *The Public* and opinion journals like it to join with the mass-produced national magazines, daily and weekly newspapers to oppose postal reform. This is ironic because much of the motivation for reforming postal practices was tied to concerns about government subsidizing advertising as opposed to regulating it.

To better understand the postal conflict in 1918, a brief history of the relationship between newspapers and the post office is helpful. U.S. postal laws between 1792 and 1873 allowed editors of newspapers to exchange copies of their papers to each other for free. According to Richard Kielbowicz, who has written extensively on U.S. postal history, this is how most newspapers gathered national news during this period. Some editors exchanged hundreds of copies of papers each week. This was particularly the case prior to the advent of the telegraph, which allowed wire services

---

145   Theodore Peterson, *Magazines in the Twentieth Century* (Urbana, Ill.: University of Illinois Press, 1956), pp. 363–364.

to expand in the mid-19th century. The 1792 postal law also allowed newspapers, no matter the size or weight, to circulate within one hundred miles or within one state for a penny. Newspapers mailed outside a state or farther than one hundred miles cost 1.5 cents in postage. During the same time, the Post Office determined postage for letters by geographic zones (how far a letter needed to go) and the number of sheets. Postage for a one-sheet letter ranged from 6 to 25 cents.[146]

The concept of a flat-rate for mailing newspapers and periodicals was in place for nearly all of the 19th century. The Mail Classification Act of 1879 continued a flat rate for periodicals and newspapers, but established four different categories for mail that is still used today. The act originated as an effort to stop marketers and publishers, who simply wanted to distribute advertising, from using the highly subsidized periodical rate. "The Post Office urged Congress to redefine the second-class mail category so that it would clearly exclude advertising sheets. Postal officials fine-tuned the legislation in consultation with leading newspaper and magazine publishers ... Despite differences, newspaper and magazine interests closed ranks with one another and with postal authorities against the so-called illegitimate periodicals, publications designed primarily for advertising purposes."[147]

The Mail Classification Act of 1879 relegated advertising to third class status, which was much more expensive. Second class postal rates were reserved for publications that were "of a public character, or devoted to literature, the sciences, arts, or some special industry, and have a legitimate list of subscribers." Second class mail cost two cents a pound to mail until 1885, then it was reduced to one cent a pound until 1917. Third class rates were one cent for two ounces, but because third class rates were paid by the piece and not in bulk the cost was about eight times as much

---

146   Kielbowicz, p. 455. See also, Richard Kielbowicz, *News in the Mail: The Press, Post Office and Public Information, 1700–1860s* (Westport, Conn.: Greenwood Press, 1989).
147   Kielbowicz, p. 456. For more on the history of the second-class mail category, see Richard B. Kielbowicz, "Origins of the Second-Class Mail Category and the Business of Policymaking, 1863–1879," *Journalism Monographs*, no. 96 (April 1986).

as second class. Given this meaningful cost difference, "publishers of all kinds" tried to qualify for the second-class rate. Postal administrators were charged with judging a publication's intent and character to decide if it was "primarily or incidentally designed for advertising purposes. The problem, as a congressional commission recognized in 1907, was that 'every periodical is designed for advertising purposes or no periodical is so designed.'"[148]

This problem led to various postal reform proposals through 1917. Between 1900 and 1917, some publishing companies challenged what they saw as arbitrary decisions by postmasters in determining what publication qualified for which rate. When in 1904 books were no longer considered second class, Houghton, Mifflin and Co. put forth a legal challenge to the Post Office's authority to make such determinations. In *Houghton v. Payne*, the U.S. Supreme Court sided with the Post Office and gave the agency wide latitude in its decision-making.[149]

In 1906, Congress created the Joint Commission of Congress on Second-Class Mail Matter to try to solve the continuing problem of Post Office deficits. Many saw the cheap second-class rates as the cause of the Post Office's chronic financial troubles. Senator Boies Penrose and Representative Jesse Overstreet headed the commission. Penrose was a Republican from Pennsylvania, known for his public criticisms of popular journalism; Overstreet was a Republican from Indiana. The commission, known as the Penrose-Overstreet Commission, proposed legislation to limit publishers' ability to inflate subscription lists, and to relegate periodicals that consisted of more than 50 percent advertising to the third class rate. In arguing the difficulty in the current construction of trying to determine, for purposes of second-class status, whether a magazine used advertising for primary or incidental purposes, the commission quoted an advertising agent in its report: "There is still an illusion to the effect that a magazine is a periodical in which advertising is incidental. But we

---

148   Kielbowicz, p. 458.
149   *Houghton v. Payne*, 194 U.S. 88 (1904). See also John E. Semonche, *Charting the Future: The Supreme Court Responds to a Changing Society, 1890–1920* (Westport, Conn.: Greenwood Press, 1978), p. 174.

don't look at it that way. A magazine is simply a device to induce people to read advertising."[150]

Newspapers and magazines vigorously objected to the commission's proposals. In the end, no action was taken and the commission asked Congress to authorize another study that would allow for the collection of additional information about operating expenses at the Post Office. When William H. Taft was elected president in 1908, he started a campaign to raise second-class rates and oversaw the first of what would become Post Office annual budget/operating reports. When Taft became president, he inherited an 89 million dollar deficit, of which about 30 percent was due to postal operations. At the time, the Post Office employed the largest number of federal employees. Through Taft's administration, he took on the challenge of postal reform and made no headway. Muckraking journalists argued that Taft was using postal reform to try to silence muckraking magazines critical of his administration. Historians believe this was a piece of Taft's agenda in pushing the reforms, and is part of the reason he failed. He was a president who did not have good relationships with the press as a whole.[151]

In 1912, when Woodrow Wilson was elected President, postal deficits had shrunk. Reform efforts now looked at linking reductions in first-class postage rates (for letters) to increases in second-class postage rates. Eventually, the House Ways and Means Committee took up the question of postal rates as part of the omnibus War Revenue Bill in 1917. That bill included a plan that involved lowering first-class rates, raising second-class rates and would initiate a postal zoning system for newspapers and periodicals that charged differently for different kinds of content. In essence, "the policy set low postal rates on the reading matter for periodicals and higher rates on advertising contents, with postage for the latter calibrated to the distance mailed."[152] The argument in favor of

---

150   Kielbowicz, p. 465.
151   Kielbowicz, pp. 469–471. See also George Juergens, *News from the White House: The Presidential-Press Relationship in the Progressive Era* (Chicago: University of Chicago Press, 1982), p. 118.
152   Kielbowicz, p. 451.

this was based partially on the idea that newspapers and magazines were profitable businesses – they received a postal subsidy that amounted to "a clear, legalized robbery by them of the people." According to the chair of the House Ways and Means Committee, the *New York Times* paid only one-fifth the actual cost of mailing its ten million pounds of newspapers each year. This was one of several examples used by the committee to illustrate the meaningful savings these large businesses recouped at the expense of the public.[153]

Newspapers, magazines and related professional interest groups joined forces to strenuously oppose the reforms, but lost the fight. On July 1, 1918 the new rates took effect. Reading matter continued to enjoy a highly subsidized flat rate of 1.25 cents in 1918, then 1.5 cents per year after that. Advertising sections, however, now paid higher rates that were graduated according to distance, and those rates rose in four steps between 1918 and 1921. When it was fully implemented, advertising matter cost a minimum of two cents to mail 150 or fewer miles, up to a maximum of ten cents for 1,800 or more miles. This is compared to a previous flat rate of one cent a pound.[154]

One of the peculiar aspects of the arguments surrounding the passage of the postal provisions in the 1917 War Revenue Act focused on the benefit of the new provisions to smaller, rural publications, mostly in the south and the west. Part of the reason the law passed was because of the support it had from lawmakers from rural areas. It was the larger, national press, which still originated mostly in the east and midwest, that was positioned to lose with the new rates.

In the early 1900s, progressives saw the national media as a way to "cultivate a sense of community among all segments of a diverse society, much as the small-town press and face-to-face communication did locally." But, by about 1912, progressives had shifted their view of the press somewhat as seen in their support of the 1912 Newspaper Act. Many progressives in 1917 supported the postal reforms because they saw mass circulation magazines and other national newspapers as purely commer-

153   Ibid, p. 473.
154   Ibid, p. 474.

cial enterprises – "just another outgrowth of a national marketing system undeserving of a public subvention."[155]

The lobbying against the implementation of the new postal regulations by the popular press showed that they also saw the new regulations as a way to impact public opinion in powerful ways that could erode national unity. The following passage in a *New York Times* column about the zoning laws illustrates the ways that the national press could aid the government in future propaganda campaigns, which emerged as an issue in 1917 with the growing advent of public relations and the creation by President Wilson of the Committee on Public Information (CPI), designed to promote the American war effort.[156]

> The tendency of the zone provisions of the new law will be to create zones of thought which will operate as a stimulant to the promotion of sectionalism, greatly to be discouraged at any time, and especially when the nation is engaged in a war for the defense of its ideals and its liberty. Artificial areas will be created and publications issued therein will have very little circulation outside. This will result in the limitation and circumscription of the interchange of expressions of public opinion and thought throughout the United States. Instead of public opinion throughout the country being a unit in its relation to the war, there will be as many divergent views as there are populous postal zones, with resulting confusion, division and dangerous conflict of opinion. The wide circulation of many publications has a broadening effect upon people in all parts of the country and tends to unite public opinion in support of Government in its measures to carry on the war.[157]

Many progressives in 1917 feared the dual nature of the mass marketed newspapers and periodicals as commercial products that not only

---

155   Ibid, p. 482.
156   Michael Schudson, *Discovering the News: A Social History of American Newspapers* (New York: Basic Books, 1978), p. 142.
157   "Postpone Zone Law, Publishers Urge: New York Association Says Radical Postal Changes will Disturb Business," *New York Times*, April 22, 1918.

conveyed information but also culture. The fight over the postal reforms was complicated because newspapers and magazines had really solidified their place as big businesses in their own right. National advertising campaigns changed the nature of the press and increased the reach of advertisers and the government to shape political, social and economic culture on a local level. And yet, the value of the national press as a vehicle to convey national information to the masses remained significant and important. While even some progressives, as evidenced in the following editorial, lament the potential impact of the postal zoning law, in many ways the law helped preserve local publications. These are the publications that the following editorial fears will get swallowed up in the growing trend toward media consolidation. The editorial highlights the complexity of the issues at the time, when threats to a free and vibrant press came as much from within as from outside.

．　．　．

Monopolizing the Press
May 11, 1918
from The Public

The union of the Chicago *Herald* with the Chicago *Examiner* is another sharp reminder of the present tendency toward the consolidation of the daily press into fewer hands. The trend is the same in large as well as small cities throughout the country. Chicago with a population of two and a half millions now has but two morning papers printed in English. Cleveland and Detroit, each with a population of over half a million, have one morning daily apiece; Indianapolis, Toledo, Columbus, Scranton, St. Paul, and New Orleans, ranging in populations from one hundred and fifty thousand to three hundred and seventy thousand, have each one morning paper. This tendency is so pronounced that some States show a decrease of nearly one half in the number of daily papers. And the movement that has been patent for a number of years has been stimulated by the present high cost of labor and materials.

In a country controlled by public opinion this change in the chief agency for molding that opinion arouses speculation as to its ultimate effect. It is highly important that the fact itself be recognized by the general public. In earlier times when the establishment of a daily paper was a matter of a small sum of money, and a few venturesome knights of the quill, every cause had its own organ; but now that such an undertaking requires millions of dollars, with little promise of dividends, the daring are deterred. This result has been brought about by the advertiser. The commercial advantage that induces venders of patent medicines to distribute free the almanacs that formerly commanded a price, caused other merchants to share the cost of publishing a newspaper for the sake of advertising their goods. Thus it came about that competition of advertisers for space, and competition of publishers for readers, reduced the price of newspapers below the cost of manufacture. The reader of a book expects to pay the whole cost of production; but the same reader would be shocked if asked to pay the cost of producing his daily newspaper.

This competition has made publishers more and more dependent upon advertisers. The big and indispensable advertisers, such as the retail merchants, and particularly the department stores, are themselves largely dependent upon the banks, and the banks in turn are controlled by great monied men who are interested directly or indirectly in securing legal privileges that are subject to public opinion. Thus the circle was completed. The citizen, called upon to vote on a traction franchise, or other delegation of public power to private individuals, looked to the great morning paper for information and counsel. The privilege seeker, aware of this fact, brought pressure to bear upon the publisher through the business department. If a big merchant hesitated to withhold advertisements from a recalcitrant publisher – in consideration of admission to the financial "deal" – a tightening of credits at the banks seldom failed to produce the desired effect. The publisher was helpless. He capitulated, or went out of business. The readers might curse him for yielding, but it never occurred to them to pay the full cost of making the paper, so that the publishers could be independent of advertisers.

Is it any wonder that the rights of the people are so rarely championed by the great dailies? No one short of a millionaire can start such a paper, or keep it going after it has been started. To oppose privileged interests means to have little advertising; to sell a paper without advertisements in competition with papers that have them, means, in the case of a metropolitan paper, a loss of from one hundred thousand to a million dollars a year. Not only have conditions rendered it impracticable to start new papers, but they have made it easy to reduce the number already in existence. The merchant finds it to his advantage to advertise in two papers with a million circulation, rather than in four with that circulation. He frowns upon a proposal to start another paper as an added expense in advertising without a corresponding benefit. Thus publishers, finding themselves ground between advancing cost of production and decreasing advertising, have no choice but to combine.

This raises the question of what is to become of that intelligent public opinion that is indispensable to a healthy democracy. Should the present tendency continue, and should the chief agencies for the distribution of news fall into the hands of a few men who are interested in sending out false reports, it may be necessary to treat the daily paper as an adjunct of the public school system, with the Secretary of State printing and distributing the paper, and with editors chosen by political parties who have space allotted them in proportion to their voting strength. Such a plan in embryo is already a part of Oregon's election machinery. The Secretary of State mails to each voter before election a pamphlet containing the laws to be voted on, together with a statement for and against them by the several political parties or organizations.

But the country has not come to that extreme. There is still a medium available for molding public opinion that will, if properly used, offer substantially the same restraint upon the consolidated press that existed during the days of more general competition. This is the weekly and monthly press, but more particularly the weekly, which occupies the field midway between the unconfirmed reports of the daily press and the philosophical dissertations of the reviews. Concentrated control of daily papers is subject to the disadvantage of arousing the readers' prejudices by the very fact of the concentration. Suspicion of unfairness causes thoughtful readers to seek some medium that is independent of central control.

This need can be met by the weekly paper. Its cost, though increasing along with other things, is still modest enough to bring it within the means of an individual or group commanding a moderate income. It comes to the reader with more personality; its editorial policy is individualized; and its judgment serves as a rule or measure with which to judge the monopoly-controlled daily.

The only escape from the consequences of ignorance lies in the increase of intelligence and wisdom on the part of citizens. The uninformed voter is ever the victim of the political adventurer. It is highly essential, therefore, that no needless obstacles be put in the way of the general circulation of the better class of weekly and monthly periodicals. There is danger, however, that this will be done if the new postal law placing newspapers on a zone basis is allowed to go into effect. Rates for merchandise should be governed by the cost of carriage, and may properly be placed on a zone basis. But newspapers are something more than merchandise. They are a medium of intelligence, a promoter of knowledge, an aid to good citizenship. The obligation that a republic should see that every citizen has proper schooling, calls also for a safe and practical means of supplying the data upon which alone the individual bases his opinion. Putting dailies on a zoning basis may not seriously handicap them because the mass of their circulation is local. But the weeklies and monthlies must from their very nature have a general circulation throughout the country, and the zoning system will be a great hardship. The publishers and members of the Associated Press who met recently in New York were right in protesting against this postal law. The press is the greatest educational force; it is indispensable to the proper functioning of democratic institutions. It should be encouraged to the widest possible circulation. Congress should modify the new postal law before it goes into effect.

Chapter 6

Moorfield Storey

To the contemporary reader, particularly one schooled in today's identity politics, the idea of a white man serving as the first president of the National Association for the Advancement of Colored People (NAACP) might appear at best improbable – at worst, a slighting of the role of African Americans in their own political and social progress. However, in 1910, to the founders of the NAACP, both black and white, Moorfield Storey was a natural choice. Sixty-four years old at the founding of the NAACP, few Americans of his day matched Storey's lifetime commitment to racial equality.

Storey's preparation for a life devoted to progressive politics and political reform began with his rearing by a father he later described as having "a brilliant mind, a marvelous memory, love of good books, and fine taste in literature," and a mother who "was a very sweet and sincere person, affectionate, modest, and indeed shy, but with a keen and well-trained mind and educated taste, a love of books, and a charming sense of humor."[158]

Born in 1845 in Roxbury, Massachusetts, Storey moved with his family to Boston when he was 11 years old, and it was as much the City of Boston, described by historian Mark Schneider as a "singular place in its attitude toward race relations during this period, producing important national leaders for the reform movement,"[159] as much as anything else in his life, that influenced the young Storey.

---

158   M.A. DeWolfe Howe, *Portrait of an Independent: Moorfield Storey 1845–1929* (Boston: Houghton Mifflin, 1932), pp. 17–19. Howe quotes from Storey's unpublished autobiography.
159   Mark Schneider, *Boston Confronts Jim Crow: 1890–1920* (Boston: Northeastern University Press, 1997), p. ix.

Family and geography laid the groundwork for the trajectory of Storey's career, beginning with the introduction his father provided that led to his first position after dropping out of Harvard Law School – a clerkship in 1867 with the staunch abolitionist Charles Sumner, chairman of the Senate Foreign Relations Committee and fellow Massachusetts native. Storey held Sumner in high esteem, writing in his 1900 biography of Sumner that the statesman's early anti-slavery speeches were "temperate but unequivocal declaration of principles (that) came with the ring of sincerity from one who thought only of his cause and not of his own fortunes."[160] The influence of Sumner on Storey lasted well past the two years he spent as Sumner's clerk, though the embodiment of a dedication to cause was not apparent to all who met the young Storey. Author Henry Adams wrote of Senator Sumner as having "as private secretary a young man named Moorfield Storey, who became a dangerous example of frivolity."[161]

Storey's future as a leader in race relations also was not apparent, even in Storey's own letters. Upon arriving in Washington to work for Sumner, he wrote to his sister Susan that "…Nothing amuses me so much here as the Negroes. Instead of Irish bootblacks, newsboys, and so forth, they are all black, and such garments as never were dreamed of in Yankee land decorate their curiously constructed frames. The little ones are as pretty as they can be, grave as our little Waverly friend, but all looking plump and healthy." He continued, "The older they grow the less attractive they become, and the less laudable their pursuits."[162] Storey's work as Sumner's personal secretary occurred during Reconstruction, when men like Sumner and the other Radical Republicans fought to guarantee civil rights to freed slaves. These men served as "living legacies to the activists of 1890 to 1920."[163]

Unlike Sumner and other political reformers to whom Storey had been exposed, Storey decided early on that he would not seek political

---

160   Moorefield Storey (John T. Morse, ed.), *American Statesman* (Boston: Houghton, Mifflin and Company, 1900), p. 51.
161   Howe, p. 39.
162   Howe, p. 43.
163   Schneider, p. 16.

office for himself. Instead, he returned to Harvard where he received his law degree in 1869. His life's focus would be on his law career and his self-appointed role of "citizen agitator." Storey rose to prominence as a lawyer in Boston. He served as editor of the *American Law Review* and was elected as president of the American Bar Association in 1896. The law, as Storey saw it, was to be used as "an instrument of reform."

According to Storey's biographer William B. Hixson, "the decisive event in Moorfield Storey's public career was the Spanish-American War."[164] The war, which began in the spring of 1898 when Storey was 53 years old, effectively ended one empire and launched another. Many historians suggest the war began as a result of the sinking of the U.S.S. Battleship Maine, which was stationed in Havana harbor to protect United States interests during the Cuban revolt against Spain. On February 15, 1898, the ship exploded and sank, killing more than three quarters of the crew. At the time, the cause of the sinking was unclear, but many in the U.S. blamed Spain.[165]

Prior to the sinking of the Maine, many in the U.S. were already urging the country toward war with Spain. In December 1897, President Grover Cleveland publicly declared that the United States might intervene in the conflict between Spain and Cuba if Spain was unable to end the crisis there. Throughout the latter part of the 19th century, Cuba struggled for independence from Spain, and the Cuban Revolutionary Party was established. The U.S. had asserted an interest in buying Cuba long before the war began in 1898. As early as 1878, U.S. sugar interests bought large tracts of land in Cuba, and by 1895 the United States had more than $50 million dollars invested in the country, and annual trade (mostly in sugar) was valued at more than $100 million.[166]

At the same time, the Philippines also began to resist Spanish rule. A call to Filipinos to revolt in 1896 was heeded; the Spanish were fighting

---

164   Howe, p. 43.
165   John M. Coward and W. Joseph Campbell, *The Indian Wars & The Spanish-American War* (Westport, Conn.: Greenwood Press, 2005), pp. 377–380.
166   Ibid.

revolutionaries in Cuba and the Philippines at the start of the Spanish-American War, and the country had just months earlier granted Puerto Rico autonomy. After President William McKinley's inauguration in March, 1898, the war effort moved forward quickly. Following the February 15 explosion of the U.S.S. Maine, Congress passed a law that allocated $50 million dollars toward a U.S. military build-up. On March 28, the U.S. Naval Court of Inquiry determined that a mine was the cause of the demise of the U.S.S. Maine, and on April 21 President McKinley ordered a blockade of Cuba. On April 23, as a result of the blockade, Spain declared war on the U.S. Two days later the U.S. declared war against Spain, and fighting began on May 1 at the Battle of Manila Bay in the Philippine Islands.[167]

Anti-Imperialism Views

It was in Storey's criticism of what he viewed as imperialistic American foreign policy that he would find new outlets for his progressive politics. He became an outspoken opponent of American occupation of the Philippines, writing numerous newspaper opinion pieces condemning what he referred to as the "electrified"[168] public reaction to battle victories in Manila Bay. Storey also condemned what he considered the disingenuous reasons for war forwarded by the federal government – "a war for liberty and human rights," as announced by the Republicans during their 1900 national convention,[169] and the growing militarism of U.S. foreign policy.

---

167   The war ended when the U.S. and Spain signed a peace treaty in Paris on December 10, 1898. The treaty established the independence of Cuba, it ceded Guam and Puerto Rico to the U.S. and allowed the U.S. to purchase the Philippine Islands from Spain for $20 million. In the end, the cost of the war to the U.S. was $250 million, and 3,000 casualties, most of which came as a result of exposure to infectious disease. For a complete look at how the press reported on the war, see Coward and Campbell, pp. 377–505.

168   Moorfield Storey, The U.S. Conquest of the Philippines (Freeport, N.Y.: Books for Libraries Press, 1926), p. 37.

169   Stuart Creighton Miller, Benevolent Assimilation: The American Conquest of the Philippines, 1899–1903 (New Haven, Conn.: Yale University Press, 1982), p. 102.

With the American press deep in the grip of yellow journalism, Storey did not have to look far to find the kind of coverage that he considered irresponsible from the very beginnings of the war – the press reports on the "sinking" of the U.S.S. Battleship Maine in Havana harbor. While the veracity of the infamous, "You furnish the pictures, and I'll furnish the war," correspondence between William Randolph Hearst and his artist in Cuba, Frederic Remington, remains unclear,[170] the newspapers were rife with headlines extolling the virtues of American conquest: "The Whole Country Thrills With War Fever," ""Havana Populace Insults the Memory of the Maine Victims," and "The Maine Was Destroyed By Treachery."[171]

Within months of the declaration of U.S. victory over the Filipino troops, Storey formed a committee of likeminded reformers to oppose American imperialism. The Anti-Imperialist League opposed U.S. annexation of the Philippines and other former Spanish colonies. In addition to Storey, the League's members included Mark Twain, President Grover Cleveland and Charles Francis Adams Jr., a direct descendant of Presidents John Adams and John Quincy Adams, and the president of the American Historical Association.[172] Adams, who worked closely with Storey, believed "that the United States had embarked on a misguided course in the wake of the Spanish-American War,"[173] diverging from what he called the "Hands-off and Walk alone" doctrine that had guided earlier U.S. international forays.

In its platform, the League contrasted the Civil War with what its members viewed as a wholly different military mission. "The real firing

---

170   Campbell, W. Joseph. "Not Likely Sent: The Remington-Hearst 'Tele-grams,'" in Journalism and Mass Communication Quarterly 77 (Summer 2000): pp. 405–422.
171   An excellent account of newspaper coverage of the Spanish-American War and the events in Cuba can be found in W.A. Swanberg, *Citizen Hearst: A Biography of William Randolph Hearst* (New York: Charles Scribner's Sons, 1961) pp. 138–139.
172   Damon W. Root, "The Part of Jefferson," *Reason* 39 (December 2007): pp. 34–39.
173   Adam Cooke, "An Unpardonable Bit of Folly and Impertinence": Charles Francis Adams Jr., American Anti-Imperialists, and the Philippines." *New England Quarterly* 83 (June 2010): pp. 313–338.

line is not the suburbs of Manila. The foe is of our own household. The attempt of 1861 was to divide the country. That of 1899 is to destroy its fundamental principles and noblest ideals."[174] U.S. involvement in both Cuba and in the Philippines was oftentimes framed in racial terms. Newspaper cartoons of the time frequently made reference to Rudyard Kipling's work *The White Man's Burden* to describe the American pursuit of bringing "civility" to foreign peoples. It was the report of atrocities by American forces against the Filipinos that brought about some of Storey's harshest criticisms. In a 1902 *New York Times* article, he is quoted: "Our soldiers are not to blame for all this. They are like the rest of their fellow citizens. Not a whit more cruel. It is the American people under false leaders which has set them to subjugate and has been content not to ask how the work was done. We at home may imitate the ostrich, but hide our heads as we may, we cannot escape our National guilt."[175] Storey believed that much of this "national guilt" was directly attributable to the press. In a 1911 letter to Woodrow Wilson, then governor of New Jersey and soon to be President of the United States, Storey spelled out his frustration with the American media.

> The American people have undertaken to govern some nine or ten millions of Asiatics thousands of miles away, and they cannot hope to do it successfully unless they can give their thought and their attention to the problem, and unless they can be furnished with the facts upon which that thought can be exercised. As a matter of fact, with very few exceptions, they know nothing and care nothing about what is going on in the Philippine Islands, and the newspapers furnish them with little or no information on the subject.[176]

The practices of late 19th and early 20th century newspapers irked Storey, and he frequently wrote letters to prominent editors and publish-

---

174   "Platform of the American Anti-Imperialist League, 1899." Platform of the American Anti-Imperialist League, 1899 (January 8, 2009): 1.
175   "Secretary Root Attacked: Anti-Imperialists Issue Circular Blaming Him Alone for Alleged Philippine Atrocities," *New York Times*, Sept 26, 1902.
176   Howe, p. 295.

ers complaining of the sensationalized reporting, invasion of personal privacy, and corrupt practices that have come to be associated with the era of yellow journalism. In an 1898 letter to the editor of the Springfield (Mass.) *Republican*, Storey wrote:

> It may be that newspapers are the most potent instrument we have to protect the people from corruption in public office and from encroachment on their rights of the corporations which control monopolies, but I am afraid that too often these monopolies control the press, and it is certain that the partisan newspaper does nothing to protect the people against the corruption of its friends but is very slow to do anything like justice to its political opponents.[177]

Storey channeled his anti-imperialist position into the role of defender of equal rights for humanity. His concern over the treatment of Filipinos seamlessly led to his work on behalf of the rights of black Americans, Native Americans and immigrants. His lifelong dedication to human rights "sprung from no sudden impulse. The early influences of anti-slavery Boston, the powerful impress of Sumner's thought, loyalty to an abstract principle of justice, and the very satisfaction of placing this loyalty above any party allegiance... "[178] Less than a decade had passed since Storey's writings against American imperialism and the nation's treatment of Filipinos when his "loyalty to justice" once again spurred him to action – this time, the acts that gained his attention were happening far closer to home.

On Aug. 14, 1908, Springfield, Illinois, home of Abraham Lincoln, erupted in a race riot that lasted two days, resulted in the near total destruction of the black parts of town, and the deaths of seven people, both black and white. The rioting began with two separate cases – one of attempted sexual assault of a white child, and the other the sexual assault of a white woman by black men. The first ended with the accused assailant slashing the throat of the father of the child. The child's father died, but not before identifying his assailant as a local black man. The

---

177   Ibid, p. 217.
178   Howe, p. 191.

second case, occurring less than a month after the first, concerned the wife of a prominent Springfield businessman being pulled from her bed and assaulted. While both cases rested on questionable evidence, they stoked anger in the white community. National newspaper coverage, while sympathetic to what they labeled the "innocent negroes," bordered on the sensationalistic. "Troops Fire Into Mob Surrounding A Dangling Body: Negro Had Been Riddled With Bullets and Then Swung to Tree..." began the front-page headline of the *St. Louis Post-Dispatch*.[179] While not the scene of the nation's first or deadliest race riot, Springfield's racial unrest resonated in popular consciousness. "Its riot presented northern publics with the startling spectacle of whites lynching blacks and burning their houses within a half mile of the Great Emancipator's homestead."[180] Historians point to the importance of the Springfield riots as a catalyst for the modern civil rights movement and the founding of the NAACP.[181] A group known as the "new abolitionists" became a driving force in an effort to respond to the violence. Journalist William English Walling of *The Independent*, New York's progressive newspaper, asked of his readers in the wake of the riots, "What large and powerful body of citizens is ready to come to [the Negro's] aid?"[182] The year following the riots, Storey attended the National Negro Conference of 1909, out of which the NAACP was formed.[183]

Storey was elected the first president of the Association, a position he would hold until his death. As president, Storey argued some of the Association's most contentious – and successful – cases. His skill as a lawyer well served the NAACP in its early legal efforts to bring about racial equality at a time when lynching and the destruction of black homes were rampant in American cities. His dedication to this cause, was, as one

---

179   Roberta Senechal de la Roche, *In Lincoln's Shadow: The 1908 Race Riot in Springfield, Illinois* (Carbondale, Ill.: Southern Illinois University Press, 1990), p. 2.
180   "4 Whites and 6 Negroes Dead, 70 Wounded In Springfield Race Riot; Militia In Control," *St. Louis Post-Dispatch*, Aug. 15, 1908.
181   Howe, p. 123.
182   "The Beginnings of The National Association for the Advancement of Colored People." 106 *New Crisis* (January 1999): p. 75.
183   Ibid.

biographer writes, "a direct reflection of the influence of Charles Sumner, who made the most notable nineteenth-century argument that the law must make no racial distinctions."[184] The early years of the NAACP, during which Storey served both as president and chief legal counsel, saw some of the Association's greatest legal successes.[185] The NAACP's first appearance before the United States Supreme Court in 1915 was in *Guinn v. U.S.*, a disenfranchisement case dealing with an Oklahoma law that exempted whites from the same voting requirements imposed on blacks, requirements that were used to exclude them from voting.[186] This case was highlighted in a memorial speech given by United States District Judge James M. Morton, Jr., in honor of Storey. [187]

> You will expect me to refer tonight to the great cases, in which Mr. Storey took a leading part, by which the rights of the colored people were upheld and established by the Supreme Court of the United States. There were three of them. The first and most important dealt with the so-called Grand-father Clause in State constitutions. A number of the Southern States, in order to disenfranchise the Negroes, amended their constitutions so that no person could vote unless he was able to read or write, or was the lineal descendent of a person entitled to vote on January 1, 1866, or of a person who on that date had resided in some foreign nation. It will be observed that this gave the suffrage to those who were entitled to it at the close of the Civil War – of course no Negro was at that time; to the descendants of such persons, which would include all Americans except Southern Negroes; and to immigrants and the descendents or immigrants. In the case which Mr. Storey backed and argued, the United States Supreme Court

---

184   Ibid, p. 99
185   Mark V. Tushnet, *The NAACP's Legal Strategy Against Segregated Education, 1925–1950* (Chapel Hill: The University of North Carolina Press, 1987). This book, while dealing mostly with the period after Storey's death, does include some of Storey's most influential legal efforts on behalf of the NAACP.
186   Ralph Cassimere Jr. "Flashback: 80 years ago the NAACP goes to court." 102 *Crisis*, 102 (1995), p. 34.
187   Mary White Ovington, *The Walls Came Tumbling Down* (New York, Schocken 1970), p. 161. See also *Guinn v. United States*, 238 U.S. 347 (1915).

declared that such provisions in State constitutions were in violation of the Constitution of the United States and were invalid. It is hard to overstate the importance of this decision to the colored people. A disfranchised people is helpless.[188]

This first case before the Supreme Court occurred the same year as the premiere of D.W. Griffith's film, *Birth of a Nation*. At a hearing to determine whether the film would be censored in Boston, both Griffith and Storey spoke. "Moorfield Storey had spoken for a few moments and as he moved to leave the platform, Griffith turned to him saying, "I am glad to have the opportunity of meeting you, Mr. Storey," and held out his hand. Storey said quietly, "I do not see why I should shake hands with you, Mr. Griffith," a delighted Mary White Ovington, a co-founder of the NAACP, recalled in her autobiography. "It was the first time, and it might be the last time that ... I would ever see a northern gentleman refuse to shake hands with a southern gentleman because he had given the country a malicious picture of the Negro."[189]

The other two cases involved a Louisville city ordinance which made it illegal for blacks to buy or move into a house on a block where whites were the majority, and a case of twelve black men whose murder convictions were handed out in a courtroom that was surrounded by a white mob. Storey's arguments were well received by the Supreme Court, which decided in favor of Storey's clients in both cases.[190] Ovington described Storey's appearance during the third case: "Moorfield Storey, white haired, clear-cut featured, the New England patrician at his finest, argued the case before the Supreme Court."

Moorfield Storey died on Oct. 24, 1929 at his farm in Lincoln, Mass., at the age of 84. He continued his writings and leadership of the NAACP up until his death. The headline of his obituary in the *New York Times* read simply "Defender of the Oppressed."[191]

---

188   This testimonial to Storey's work on behalf of civil rights can be found in Howe, p. 256.
189   Ovington, p. 129.
190   Howe, pp. 256–257.
191   "Moorfield Storey, Leader of Bar, Dies," *New York Times (1923–Current file);* Oct 25, 1929, p. 27.

Storey's Vision for the Press

Storey's ideas about war and the role the press played in fueling conflict and unduly influencing public opinion in pro-war ways developed during the Spanish-American War at the end of the 19th century, but also informed his thoughts about how the daily press covered World War I. The United States entered the war in 1917. By the time Storey wrote the following article, which appeared in 1922 in the *Atlantic Monthly*, Storey believed that war was not the solution to world problems. He continued to advocate for peace, and to scold the press for "exciting hostilities," and for pandering to demands for sensationalized news. Storey heralded the power of the press and offered a sentiment that many media critics still articulate today – an appeal for press responsibility and a return to guiding press values that serve public discourse and democracy and not profit maximization. As Storey notes in the following article, the news "is a great educational force for good or evil, and those who conduct the press, while they exercise its power, should recognize their responsibility."

· · ·

The daily press
By *Moorfield Storey*[192]

There never was a time in the history of the world when greater problems pressed for solution than now. The relations between nations are critical, and the hatreds engendered by the recent war are fraught with infinite dangers. Shall we attempt to make war impossible? Shall we cease to bankrupt ourselves by making preparation for hostilities, or shall we make no effort to protect civilization against another world-conflict? What can we do to equalize the conditions of men, restore cor-

---

192   Moorfield Storey, "The daily press," *The Atlantic Monthly* (January 1922).

dial relations between employer and employee? How shall we deal with the racial ill-feeling that is responsible for lynching, Ku Klux Klans, and multiform lawlessness? What is the remedy for the corruption and inefficiency that are so common in legislative bodies and among public officials? How adjust the crushing burdens of taxation, how provide for adequate transportation of goods and passengers? These are a few of the questions that demand attention.

The newspaper press is the source from which the public derives its knowledge of the facts. The daily journal goes into every home, every office, and every workshop. It can educate the people by its comments on events as they occur, and by its discussion of public questions. It asserts for itself a great position as the 'Fourth Estate.' It claims for itself great rights and great privileges – practically unrestrained free speech and reduced postage, among others. Its powers and its privileges carry with them great responsibilities, for it can lead or mislead the public. It is bound to lay before its readers only the truth, and, in printing the news, to remember that what it lays before its readers should be only 'that which is fit to print.' It is a great educational force for good or evil, and those who conduct the press, while they exercise its power, should recognize their responsibility.

When this view is presented to editors, they are apt to remind us that a newspaper is a commercial enterprise; that it must secure adequate circulation, or die; that, to gain circulation, it must publish what its readers wish to see; and that it cannot take a higher stand than its readers permit. In adopting this rule, the editor, of course, abandons to a great extent his position as leader. His readers lead him, not he his readers. If a strong editorial on some question in which people are warmly interested brings many letters of condemnation or threats of discontinuing subscriptions, and he yields to these critics, it is they, not he, who edit his newspapers. The press must either lead or follow; and, if it follows by catering to a depraved public taste or a popular prejudice, it is largely responsible for the taste or prejudice, for both grow by what feeds them. To every editor is presented the question: 'Shall I seek money through increased circulation and advertisements, or shall I try to create a sound public opinion and make my journal a power for good?'

The public demand for certain kinds of news ought not to be the guide. The majority of men may enjoy scandals, the evidence in divorce suits or murder trials, the details of investigations into unsavory crimes. So also would they enjoy knowing what the incomes of their neighbors are, whether their domestic relations are happy, whether the business of each is making or losing, what diseases or infirmities affect them. Prurient curiosity has no limits; but the press cannot justify the invasion of private life by the claim that its readers like it. The competition between newspapers tends steadily to lower the bars that protect the private citizen against impertinent curiosity; and it is the duty of every editor who recognizes his responsibility as a leader to resist this tendency.

How, at this crisis, in the world's affairs, does the press meet it? A few weeks ago, in California, a man named Arbuckle was charged with a crime. The details of the investigation that followed were loathsome. If any guest at the table of a decent family had related the story in the presence of the wife and children of his host, he would have been expelled from the house, and never again admitted. No gentleman would for a moment have made the case a subject of conversation with a lady; no lady would have permitted it. Yet the daily newspapers, with a few honorable exceptions, gave a prominent place to every detail of the case for some days, and laid them thus before men, women, and children for whose eyes they were unfit. The editors thus brought into every home a story which, as gentlemen, they would never have told there in person. Can this be justified? Cannot a newspaper observe the ordinary rules of decent society? What possible good could this publication do anybody?

This is merely an instance. A leading Boston newspaper not long ago had, in a single issue, parts of six columns devoted to as many different divorce cases – not even local news, but collected from other states. The Stillman scandal, the Stokes case,[193] and many others are forced upon

---

193   The Stillman scandal involved a high profile divorce proceeding between the president of National City Bank and his wife, whom he alleged had a child out of wedlock. The paternity of their 2-year-old child was part of the extensive reporting on the divorce proceedings. The Stokes case was a high-profile

our attention day after day. In these cases the public has no legitimate interest. They are calamities to the parties concerned, and sore afflictions to the children and relatives and close friends of the parties. The publication of all the evidence only increases the burden which the children must bear through life. The first glance at our morning paper reveals a catalogue of crimes, of accidents, of scandals, which make us sick. What education do the people get from these chronicles? What is the leadership which prompts such a selection of news? We all know that offenses must come; but 'woe unto him by whom the offense cometh' to our own tables every morning. The decent people of a community have some rights, and should not be compelled to wade through tales of commonplace crime and filthy scandal every morning and evening.

There is another important respect in which the press fails. The relations between nations now are strained in many ways, and it is the duty of everyone to use his influence for peace. War is unthinkable. If we have already forgotten the horrors through which we lived for more than four years, the devastated regions, the hideous barbarities, the frightful loss of life; if the green graves of those we loved, the shattered lives of blind, maimed, and disabled men, no longer touch us, the crushing burden of taxation, which even our little part in the war has placed upon our backs, will not let us forget it. Can we think without horror of new drafts upon our youth, new slaughter, new drives to sell bonds and raise moneys to relieve suffering of every kind, new profiteers, higher prices of food and raiment, more of all the horrors that we can remember if we will?

Yet the newspapers talk glibly of the next war. Instead of keeping out of their columns all appeals to prejudice against England, France, Germany, Japan, Mexico, and other countries, they are constantly publishing, now editorials appealing to prejudice or fostering suspicion, now letters from persons who, profoundly ignorant of the facts, speak confidently of English hostility or greed, of Japanese craft and ambition, of French selfishness. They let men who have traveled briefly in other

---

murder case in which author Edward Stokes was accused of gunning down wealthy playboy James Fisk in the Grand Central Hotel in New York City. Supposedly at the center of the murder was the affection of a Broadway starlet.

countries spread at length their hasty conclusions from isolated experiences about people whose language they did not speak and could not understand. They scatter recklessly sparks that at any moment may explode a magazine or kindle a conflagration. One set, at the behest of exploiting interests, would embroil us with Mexico. Another insists that war for the control of the Pacific is inevitable; as if that ocean, to use Mr. Lowell's phrase, could be anybody's 'backyard.' Other so-called patriots hope to involve us in war with England, because they would have Ireland independent, heedless of the consequences which such a war would entail upon civilization. Because a portion of four millions of people want to govern themselves, perhaps as they govern some of our great cities, they would bring on a life-and-death struggle between hundreds of millions of men, who for every reason in the world should be friends. Their attempts to excite hostilities, in the form of letters and speeches, find ready access to the columns of the daily press. This is criminal recklessness, and the editors should remember Bismarck's words: --

'Every country is held at some time to account for the windows broken by its press. The bill is presented some day or other in the form of hostile sentiment in the other country.'

Why do not those who guide our newspapers tell us what is good in our fellow beings? There is no lack of material, and there are beams in our own eyes. Why don't they do all that they can to discourage national prejudice, to make men realize what war would mean? Why don't they use their great power to lead the people in the paths of peace? They call themselves Christian, and they ignore the fundamental truth that we should love, not hate, our neighbors. Can they not rise to some appreciation of Garrison's noble utterance: 'My country is the world, my countrymen are all mankind'?

Instead of filling pages with incessant harping on some worn-out joke, like the powerful Katrinka, and hideous colored pictures; instead of page after page devoted to sports, adorned by portraits of boys and men who are members of some team, why not educate readers to something better than sport? The facts which underlie labor unrest could be studied carefully and published, greatly to the benefit of us all. The real incidence of taxation, and how the burden can best be distributed, would interest a suffering public. What portion of our expense is waste, and where we practice undue economy, is a fertile subject, where careful study would lead to constructive suggestion. The truth on matters of real public interest, well-weighted advice, -- the news that is fit to print, -- are what we have a right to expect from our newspapers; and if our expectation, our reasonable demands, were met, the press would be a great power for good, and would lead the public up. To-day it is abandoning its high place, and, so far from educating the people, is too often corrupting and debasing them.

To this appeal, which they recognize as containing much truth at least, the editors reply, "But if we adopt your policy, we cannot sell our newspapers."

The answer is that to-day there are journals which do not print scandals, or make of their columns a Newsgate Calendar; which do not waste paper, now so dear, upon senseless colored vulgarities and the portraits of nonentities, and yet command a large circulation. There is a demand for more such papers.

The *Tribune* under Horace Greeley, the *Evening Post* under Bryant, the Boston *Advertiser* in its palmy days, were edited with a purpose and won public support. Examples could be given from among the journals of to-day. A newspaper well edited, and appealing to the best and not the worst that is in us, -- a Springfield *Republican* on a larger scale, and published in a metropolitan centre; a Manchester *Guardian* occupying in America the place which that newspaper fills in England, -- would not lack adequate support. All our newspapers can come nearer to these high examples by at least excluding from their columns the matter that appeals to the lowest prejudices and passions of their readers. They may not become great leaders, but they can at least not be demagogues and scandal-mongers. Is not the experiment worth trying?

If it is not, we shall learn to regard a free press, not as a priceless boon, but as a necessary evil.

Chapter 7

Oswald Garrison Villard, The Nation and Atlantic Monthly

According to historians, journalists, friends and family of Oswald Garrison Villard, two strains, prominent in the history of the later 19th and early 20th centuries, ran strongly through his life – capitalist expansion and humanitarian reform. Although these two strains seem incompatible, they ultimately resulted in Villard becoming a prominent liberal, journalist and activist. The wealth with which he lived did not push him away from humanitarian causes. Villard embraced the concept of *noblesse oblige*, the idea that those in the privileged class should work to have their privileges extended to others. Writing in the 1920s, Villard lamented that the European notion of *noblesse oblige* did not exist in the United States, and that wealth should bring with it a sense of responsibility and readiness to serve the state and country.[194]

Most credit Villard's liberal beliefs to his parents – his strong anti-imperialism views; his staunch support for civil rights, free speech and press and pacifism; and, his efforts toward advancing women's suffrage and rights for African Americans. Oswald Garrison Villard was the son of Ferdinand Heinrich Gustave Hilgard and Helen Frances (Fanny) Garrison, the daughter of famous abolitionist William Lloyd Garrison. He was born in Germany in 1872 during one of his parents' trips abroad.[195]

In 1853, Villard's father immigrated to New York to avoid being forced

---

194   D. Joy Humes, *Oswald Garrison Villard, Liberal of the 1920's* (Syracuse, N.Y.: Syracuse University Press, 1960); Michael Wreszin, *Oswald Garrison Villard, Pacifist at War* (Bloomington, Ind.: Indiana University Press, 1965); Gilbert Murray, *Liberality and Civilization* (London: George Allen, Ltd., 1938), p. 31.

195   Humes, p. 1; Wreszin, pp. 7–10.

into the German Army by his father. He changed his name to Henry Villard to avoid his father finding him. Villard had been well educated in Germany, and spent his first few years in the U.S. working as an editor at a German language newspaper and as a teacher. He lived in Illinois, Wisconsin and Pennsylvania.[196]

By 1858, he had landed a job as a correspondent for the *New York Staats-Zeitung*, another German language newspaper, and caught the attention of English language newspapers for his reporting on the Lincoln-Douglas debates. He eventually mastered writing in English, and by 1860 was covering the presidential campaign for *The Cincinnati Commercial*, the St. Louis *Missouri-Democrat* and the *New York Tribune*. Villard became a famous war correspondent for *The Chicago Tribune* during the Civil War, and also worked as a foreign correspondent for the *New York Tribune*.[197]

During Villard's trip to Germany in 1872 to cover the Austro-German War for the *New York Tribune*, Oswald Garrison Villard was born, and the beginning of Henry's wealth and power took seed. On that visit, Henry Villard became associated with the German stockholders of the Oregon and California Railroad Company. During the rest of the 1870s, his interest in transportation grew, and eventually Villard emerged as a powerful railroad financier. In less than a decade, he had created and become the president of the Oregon Railway and Navigation Company, the Oregon Improvement Company, the Oregon Transcontinental Company and numerous other investment and development corporations. In 1881, he bought control of the Northern Pacific Railroad. He also purchased the *New York Evening Post* and its weekly supplement, *The Nation*, both of which his son would eventually inherit. In 1893, Villard bought the Edison Lamp Company and the Edison Machine Works, which many years later would evolve into the General Electric Company. At the time of his death in 1900, Henry Villard was remembered as a "war correspondent and newspaper owner, railroad financier and promoter of the practical

---

196   Ibid.
197   Henry Villard, *Memoirs of Henry Villard, Journalist and Financier, 1835–1900* (2 vols, Boston, 1904); Wreszin, pp. 7–10.

application of electricity."[198]

While his father had influence on Villard during his formative years, one historian suggests, "It is impossible to overestimate the influence Villard's mother had in shaping his personality."[199] Fanny Garrison Villard was a passionate advocate for the rights of women and blacks, and was an outspoken pacifist. She was the president of the Women's Peace Society between 1919 and 1928, and she was an active member of the National Association for the Advancement of Colored People (NAACP) and the Woman Suffrage Association.[200]

In his memoirs, Oswald Garrison Villard wrote about how his parents' backgrounds and ideas shaped his views about the world: "These were the divergent strains which made me what I am. These were the parents who gave me every opportunity in life, every benefit that wealth could bestow and forged the tools that I used in my effort to mold the public opinion of my time."[201]

Villard's efforts to mold "the public opinion of [his] time," began after his graduate studies at Harvard. Villard was headed down an academic path, but much to his father's disappointment, he decided on a career in journalism instead of a Ph.D. With the help of his father, he got a job at the *Philadelphia Press.* His time there lasted about six months. Villard later noted that the *Press* was good training because it "was a perfect example of what a newspaper should *not* be: it truckled to its advertisers and bowed to social pressure; its reporters were apathetic and cynical, and its editorial policy was devoted to none of the aims of responsible journalism."[202]

In 1897, Villard took a job for his father at the *New York Evening Post* at a time when the *Post* was "engaged in one of its crusades." The paper was "opposed to the exploitation of the revolutionary situation in Cuba," and argued that the U.S. had no right to interfere. In every major inci-

---

198 Humes, pp. 3–4.
199 Wreszin, p. 9.
200 Humes, p. 7.
201 Oswald Garrison Villard, *Fighting Years: Memoirs of a Liberal Editor* (New York: Harcourt, Brace & Co., 1939), p. 23.
202 Wreszin, p. 18.

dent leading up to the Spanish American War in 1898, the *Post* took the side of Spain. Even after the U.S.S. Maine was sunk, the *Post* editorials insisted there was no proof that Spain was responsible. It maintained its position against U.S. involvement well into the war.[203]

As the war progressed, Villard became a strong opponent of what he considered to be the Roosevelt strategy of using war as a means to acquire strategic foreign territory for the United States. By the summer of 1898, Villard was an active member of the American Anti-Imperialist League, whose other prominent members included philosopher John Dewey, Moorfield Storey and Edwin Lawrence Godkin, co-founder of *The Nation* in 1865 and an editor with whom Villard worked at both the *Post* and *The Nation*.

Between 1897 and 1918, Villard was an activist, a writer, and a businessman. When his father died in 1900 he inherited the *Post* and *The Nation*, but Villard did not assume editorship of *The Nation* until 1918, after he sold the *Evening Post*. Among the books he wrote during this time are *The Early History of Wall Street* (1897), *John Brown: A Biography Fifty Years After* (1910), and *Germany Embattled* (1915). In addition to publishing books and writing for his own publications (the *Post* and *The Nation*), Villard also served as a contributing writer to *Century*, *Scribner's*, *Harper's*, *Forum*, *Christian Century*, *Progressive* and other important journals.

In terms of his activism, this time period saw Villard become an important member of several organizations. He was a leader in the American Anti-Imperialist League, and worked to organize a third-ticket candidate for the 1900 presidential election. Ultimately, they were unsuccessful in winning the presidency. In 1909, Villard wrote the call for a conference of blacks and whites that would lead to the formation of the National Association for the Advancement of Colored People (NAACP). He helped the NAACP in a variety of ways – he gave the group free space to meet in the *Evening Post* building; the *Post* gave the association a lot of favorable coverage and refused to publish stories that reflected unfavorably

---

203   Ibid.

on the "Negro cause;" and, Villard gave the NAACP generous financial support. During this time, Villard also financially supported the Urban League and the Civil Liberties Union.[204] Historian Michael Wreszin notes the importance of Villard to the NAACP:

> His name, coupled with his energy and organizational ability, did much to build the Association's firm foundation and for the first five years of its existence he was a dominant figure. He served as disbursing treasurer and as chairman of the board. The ridicule he received in the press for his frequent public appearances at biracial dinners and organizing conventions in no way dampened his ardor. Although he later resigned his chairmanship because he found it difficult to share authority with William E.B. DuBois, editor of *The Crisis*, he remained a prominent member throughout his life. The general failure of progressives to deal with the Negro problem in 1912 presented a glaring gap in their reform ideology and it took a good deal of courage on Villard's part to openly dedicate himself to their cause; the same kind of courage that it took to parade down Fifth Avenue for women's suffrage.[205]

In 1912, Villard publicly supported Woodrow Wilson for President of the United States. He believed that Wilson would advance "Negro rights" and would institute women's suffrage. But, after Wilson's election, Villard was disappointed that Wilson chose instead to support policies of segregation. He attracted Wilson's ire when he used Wilson's own writings about democracy in *The New Freedom* to criticize the president. Villard noted that nowhere in Wilson's writings "do we find any indication that his democracy is not strictly limited by the sex line and the color line."[206] Villard was even angrier at the administration when blacks were called upon to help fight for the U.S. in World War I. "What hypocrisy! What

---

204   Humes, pp. 76–79.
205   Wreszin p. 30–31.
206   Villard, p. 240. See also Ray Stannard Baker, *Woodrow Wilson: Life and Letters* (Garden City, N.Y.: Doubleday & Co., Inc., 1931), Vol. III, pp. 221–22.

injustice! They were forced to die for the country which was still for them what Wendell Phillips had called it in Abolition days, 'a magnificent conspiracy against justice!'"[207]

In 1918, Villard devoted most of his time to *The Nation*. On February 1, 1918, Villard was owner, publisher and editor of *The Nation* and served in this capacity until 1932. Villard's *Nation* saw record circulation – in his first two years as editor, readership grew from 7,200 to more than 38,000. According to historian Dollena Joy Humes, *The Nation* and *The New Republic* became influential voices of American liberalism between 1918 and 1932. Villard, unlike many liberals during this time, steadfastly held to his anti-war beliefs.

In addition to maintaining his interest in fighting for civil rights, Villard was also someone who scrutinized his own profession. He was a vocal critic of newspapers he thought were unduly influenced by advertisers, and he was concerned about the "disappearing daily" newspaper, which he felt was vulnerable to the trend of news as a "great business enterprise."[208]

Villard published several articles and books about journalism. One of his columns about newspaper consolidation appears in the next chapter. In 1923, Villard wrote *Some Newspapers and Newspaper-Men* about the status of American journalism at the time. The book included a thoroughly researched history of the press that drew from his training as a historian at Harvard. He revised and updated his 1923 study and reprinted it in 1926 under the same title. Then, in 1944 Villard issued a new edition of the book that included his thoughts about some of the more significant challenges of journalism. Included in the 1944 book, entitled *The Disappearing Daily, Some Chapters in American Newspaper Evolution*, were chapters on free speech and press and the relationship of the press with the President. The book also addressed the challenges that radio brought to journalism as a new mass medium. In the book's preface, Villard writes about the importance of the press in ways that reflect his own long history as a writer, publisher and activist.

---

207   Villard, p. 241.
208   Oswald Garrison Villard, *The Disappearing Daily, Some Chapters in American Newspaper Evolution* (New York: Alfred Knopf, 1944), p. v.

The slow disappearance of the American daily is doubly a menace: not only does it tend to deprive the people of vital information, it even threatens if it continues, to bring nearer governmental supplying and control of news, under which republican institutions could not possibly flourish. It is of the utmost importance, therefore, that every newspaper development be scrutinized and weighed with the greatest care if only because of the danger that our dailies will be more and more controlled by individuals of enormous wealth, committed to the preservation of the *status quo* because of their material prosperity. One can only hope at this hour that out of the present turmoil and struggle, and those which are inevitable in the coming reconstruction period, there will again emerge brave and dauntless spirits to bring about a renaissance of the trade of imparting the news, coupled with the offering of moral and spiritual leadership, as has happened in the past, notably in anti-slavery days.[209]

Villard died in 1949, and history has recorded him as one of the best-known political journalists in the United States between 1918 and 1932, predominantly because of his work at *The Nation*. The causes he supported in the first half of the 20th century were most of the great controversies of the time, and Villard was one of the few outspoken, crusading liberals of his time. Humes notes that he was "an acute observer of the world of which he was a part; he was an interpreter of the political and social scene; and he attempted to correct the political and social evils or abuses of his day. In so doing, he did much to define and defend the liberal position of the 1920s."[210]

The Atlantic Monthly

Villard's *Nation* was one of several magazines of the time known for the advocacy of progressive ideals, but it was both *The Nation* and the *Atlantic Monthly* – whose founding predated *The Nation's* by nine years

---

209   Villard, p. vi.
210   Humes, p. 14.

– that stood out for their unflinching coverage of politics and culture. Another commonality is that they have both survived, unlike many of their contemporaries. While the history of American political and literary magazines can be traced as far back as 1741 with the launch of Benjamin Franklin's *General Magazine* and Andrew Bradford's *American Magazine*,[211] it took more than another hundred years for the industry to find the catalyst that would unleash what historians have called the "great explosion"[212] in magazine publication and circulation – the uneasy years just preceding the Civil War. The talk of war, and later the war itself, allowed the newly established periodicals to inundate the increasingly literate American public with news and opinion. Among the most important (measured by both influence and endurance) were the *Atlantic Monthly* and *The Nation*. Both magazines played a large role – particularly within intellectual circles – in framing views of history, both for Progressive Era readers and today's historians.

A group identified as "Yankee humanists,"[213] including Oliver Wendell Holmes, Ralph Waldo Emerson, and the magazine's first editor, James Russell Lowell, founded the *Atlantic Monthly* in 1857. "The Founding of the *Atlantic Monthly*...marked [the] high tide of the Boston mind," wrote Van Wyck Brooks in his 1915 book *America's Coming of Age*.[214] The founders were keenly aware of their cultural responsibility and believed "...that the democratic age indeed needed intellectual, moral, and aesthetic leadership and that the magazine should contribute to that cultural leadership by addressing itself to the 'discerning minority,' which in turn could educate the tastes of the broader majority."[215] Just as the men who founded the

---

211   Tom Huntington, "THE MAGAZINE WORLD." 44 *Civil War Times* (2005): pp. 16–59.
212   John William Tebbel and Mary Ellen Zuckerman, *The Magazine in America, 1741–1990* (New York: Oxford University Press, 1991).
213   Ellery Sedgwick, *The Atlantic monthly, 1857–1909: Yankee Humanism at High Tide and Ebb.* (Amherst, Mass.: University of Massachusetts Press, 1994).
214   Van W. Brooks, *America's Coming-of-Age: By Van Wyck Brooks* (New York: The Viking Press, 1915), p. 21.
215   Sedgwick, p. 26.

Atlantic,[216] the magazine itself was "explicitly a product of New England, and the magazine became as much an organ for the export of New England conscience as for New England literary culture."[217]

The magazine, while welcoming of diverse opinions and differing literary tastes, was staunchly anti-slavery. A piece in the December 1857 edition made clear the editors' opinions of the South. "That the intelligent and civilized portion of a race should consent to the sway of their illiterate and barbarian companions in the commonwealth … is an astonishment that should be a hissing to all beholders everywhere."[218] The decades between the founding of the *Atlantic* and the Progressive Era, while a period of growth for the magazine, saw little departure in content; it continued in its idealistic aims of being a civilizing influence on its readership and society. With the elevation of Walter Hines Page to the editorship in 1898, the magazine became decidedly more political and in line with what has come to be known as the "progressive publishing movement."[219] Page was "impatient to jettison much of the *Atlantic's* baggage of high culture to gain present-day impact and broader influence."[220]

Page's successor, Bliss Perry, whose editorials criticized militaristic nationalism (including colonization in the Philippines) and took on issues of race and disenfranchisement, invited contributions from writers including W.E.B. Du Bois and H.G. Wells.[221] Beginning with Page, and further encouraged by Perry, Du Bois wrote many pieces for the *Atlantic* on the lives of black Americans. Many of these stories served as the foundation for his first book, *The Souls of Black Folk*.[222] "Some of the

---

216   For an in-depth biography of each of the magazine's founders, see M.A. DeWolfe Howe, *The Atlantic Monthly and Its Makers* (Boston: The Atlantic Monthly Press, 1919).
217   Ibid, p. 62.
218   Taken from the Dec. 1857 edition of the *Atlantic*, quoted in Sedgwick, p. 62.
219   The progressive era in publishing is discussed at length in Christopher Wilson, *The Labor of Words: Literary Professionalism in the Progressive Era* (Athens: University of Georgia Press, 1985).
220   Sedgwick, p. 276.
221   Ibid, p. 304, 307.
222   Sedgwick, p. 269, 316.

sketches appeared first in the *Atlantic Monthly* and were so poignant, so terribly sincere that McClurg, a Chicago publisher, asked Du Bois for a book."[223] It was in Perry's *Atlantic* that Du Bois first voiced in print his call for higher education opportunities for blacks.[224] "Since its first 1857 edition, critics have seen the influential and respected *Atlantic* as a fount of probity, literary brilliance, and liberal progressivism."[225]

Perry's tenure as the *Atlantic's* editor "corresponded with the era of muckraking, a critical reevaluation of the excesses of the gilded age and the rise of corporate America,"[226] as well as "a sharp upsurge in popular theories of Anglo-Saxon superiority and manifest destiny."[227] His liberal humanist politics along with his pragmatic ideas of what made magazines of the day sell, led Perry to engage the writers and editors of the *Atlantic* with more contemporary issues. His desire "to make humanistic culture more engaged in the present,"[228] – and to keep the *Atlantic* financially afloat – led Perry to keep the magazine's content contemporary.

> If the *Atlantic Monthly* were a repository; if it confined itself to the discussion of Roman antiquities, or the sonnets of Wordsworth, or the planning of the colony of Massachusetts Bay, no one but the specialists would concern themselves with the opinions expressed in its pages. But it happens to be particularly interested in this present world; curious about the actual conditions of politics and society, of science and commerce, of art and literature. Above all, it is engrossed with the lives of the men and women who are making America what it is and is to be.[229]

---

223   Mary White Ovington, *The Walls Came Tumbling Down* (New York: Schocken Books, 1970), p. 54.
224   Sedgwick, p. 308.
225   Michael E. Chapman, "Pro-Franco Anti-communism: Ellery Sedgwick and the *Atlantic Monthly*," 41 *Journal of Contemporary History* (2006): pp. 641-662.
226   Sedgwick, p. 303.
227   Ibid, p. 309.
228   Ibid, p. 281.
229   Howe, p. 97.

Perry's departure from the editorship of the magazine in 1909 coincided with a re-organization of the *Atlantic's* business model under Ellery Sedgwick, who would remain as editor for the next 30 years. Under Sedgwick, the magazine began publishing as a part of the newly established Atlantic Monthly Company, which also published books through the Atlantic Monthly Press. It further expanded with the acquisition of other magazines, including *House Beautiful*.[230] "For the first time since the days of James T. Fields (the magazine's second editor), the editor was directly concerned with the publishing success of the magazine."[231] Sedgwick further emphasized progressive journalism, somewhat to the detriment of the *Atlantic's* literary heritage. This escalation of Perry's earlier desire for the magazine to cover more contemporary topics, resulted in a surge in readership. These changes brought the *Atlantic*, both for better and for worse, closer to the commercial mainstream of American culture."[232]   While Perry's political leanings and cultural aesthetic (in large degree shared by Sedgwick) certainly were reflected in the content of the *Atlantic* during his tenure, "he did not attempt to make (it) an organ for his own opinions."[233]

Villard and *The Nation*

The same could not be said for Villard and his *Nation*. While editor, he successfully embraced both *The Nation's* mission at its founding to, "not be the organ of any party, sect, or body,"[234] and his abolitionist grandfather William Lloyd Garrison's ideas about an editor's role, as proclaimed in the masthead of Garrison's *Liberator* nearly 90 years earlier: "I am in earnest – I will not equivocate – I will not excuse – I will not retreat a single inch – and I *will be heard*."[235]

---

230   Howe, p. 97–98.
231   Ibid.
232   Sedgwick, p. 314.
233   Sedgwick, p. 304.
234   From *The Nation's* founding prospectus, as reproduced at www.the-nation.com.
235   William Lloyd Garrison, 1831, in Lewis Gannett, "Villard's *Nation*," 171

And heard Villard was. In 2000, *The Nation* published a timeline of its own history under the title, *"The Nation*: An Alternative History," in which it noted that when Oswald Garrison Villard became editor in 1918, "the political perspective [of the magazine] shifted radically."[236] When Villard turned his full attention to *The Nation*, he made it a reflection of himself. The magazine was transformed within months of Villard's leadership, becoming one of the most influential liberal weeklies in the country and challenging *The New Republic* as a serious rival. As Villard biographer Michael Wreszin writes, *The Nation's* "point of view became a rallying point for a number of brilliant young writers who were to be prominent in the field of journalism ... for years to come."[237]

When Villard took the helm of the magazine in 1918, he already had a plan in place to promote peace and an end to World War I. He also decided to take President Woodrow Wilson to task for his "neglect of civil liberties." In continuing to write in *The Nation* about Wilson's policies that Villard believed violated many civil rights, he "had struck upon a weakness of the President." Many of Wilson's early supporters were not in favor of the war, and they had grave concerns about the way the president was dealing with civil liberties at home during the war. *The Nation* exploited this weakness in its weekly columns.[238]

Villard's outspoken criticism of President Wilson and his war policies earned him and the magazine the attention of the Federal Bureau of Investigation (FBI). In a 1986 article published by *The Nation* that detailed the magazine's long history of F.B.I. surveillance, Villard was featured prominently. The article noted that the F.B.I. was watching Villard because of his anti-war sentiments. Among other things, his file noted that he was of German ancestry. Also within the F.B.I's files on Villard were many copies of *The Nation*. Some of the earliest copies were connected to the controversial 1920 murder case against two Italian immigrants in Massachusetts – Nicolas Sacco and Bartolomeo Vanzetti.

The Nation (July 22, 1950), p. 79.

236   *The Nation: An Alternative History*, 270 (Jan. 10, 2000): pp. 8–51.

237   Wreszin, p. 90.

238   Ibid, p. 94.

Many people questioned the guilt of the two men and suggested that they did not get a fair trial. The F.B.I. files on Villard suggest that the agency was investigating whether *The Nation* "is also distributing Sacco-Vanzetti propaganda."[239]

Handwritten notes in the file also offered the following about the magazine during the early 1920s when it was being watched: "In 1920 Samuel Gompers former pres of A F of L[240] denounced *The Nation* as being un-American & of Bolshevist tendency," and "In 1921 Ernest H. Gruening was Managing Editor of *The Nation*. Criticized use of Marines in Haiti. Gruening is a former member of the Commt vs American Imperialism."[241] Many other entries were noted, and all of them suggested that the magazine's stances against the president's policies and actions were worthy of watching by the F.B.I.[242]

Writings from Oswald Garrison Villard and his *Nation* are excerpted in the next chapter. They show Villard's concern about two primary influences that sought to silence dissenting and minority voices – media consolidation and government censorship. The extensive F.B.I. file on Villard and his magazine suggest that his concerns over growing restrictions on freedom of speech and press were not unfounded.

---

239   Penn Kimball, "The History of *The Nation*, According to the F.B.I.," *The Nation* (March 22, 1986), pp. 399–426.
240   AFL stands for the American Federation of Labor.
241   Ibid, p. 400.
242   The use of the term Bolshevist means someone who supported the Bolshevik Party in Russia, led by Vladimir Lenin in 1917. The Bolshevik Revolution led to the overthrow of the Russian government.

Chapter 8

Threats to a Free Press:
Media Consolidation and Censorship

What is the purpose of the press? While entertainment as a function of the American newspaper is traced back to colonial times, the roots of U.S. journalism are tied to political discourse and contributing to the health and function of a democracy. Between 1783 and 1801, the most notable feature of journalism was its attachment to the political parties. The daily newspaper emerged in 1783, and by the turn of the century newspapers were spreading across America, largely because of the freedom enjoyed by the press in post-revolutionary times. "Greater freedom of comment and wider range of debatable topics were characteristic of this new and rather wild journalism."[243]

Throughout the 19th century, journalism would see substantial change. In the 1880s, charismatic publishers like Joseph Pulitzer would alter the way newspapers thought about and produced news. Newspaper historian Frank Luther Mott writes that Pulitzer did more "toward setting the pattern of modern journalism than anyone else" by keeping important and significant news as the backbone of his publications, while also scouring a city for gossip and news items that could be sensationalized. Pulitzer believed strongly in the importance of the editorial page, and championed many liberal ideas of the time. He believed that the editorial page should help in the formation of public opinion and took this responsibility seriously. He also added more pages to the paper and became a leader in newspaper illustration. His new approach took hold because Pulitzer's papers were showing strong circulation gains and favorable

---

243   Frank Luther Mott, *American Journalism, A History: 1690–1960* (3rd Ed.) (New York: The MacMillan Company, 1966), p. 143.

responses from the public. Many others copied his approach as a result.[244]

This new trend toward sensationalizing the news morphed into what many call "yellow journalism," which lasted from about 1886 through the turn of the century. William Randolph Hearst is most commonly credited with creating yellow journalism, which included the practice of using excessively large headlines that screamed excitement, often about crime or scandal stories; the "lavish" use of photographs, including many that were not of real events, but rather staged; the inclusion of fake interviews in the paper and of the publication of stories about pseudo-science; the inclusion of comics in the Sunday papers; and, writing stories about the "underdog" that included campaigns for action against the abuses suffered by common people.[245]

As noted in chapters three and five, it was also during this time that the role advertising played in the newspaper would increase substantially. Because of the changes to both its content and its business structure, newspapers flourished. Famous editor Arthur Brisbane observed in 1904, "Journalistic success brings money. The editor has become a money man. Where your treasure is, your heart will be also."[246] The newspaper of the early 20th century had progressed over more than a century from serving as a platform for partisan propaganda to private one-man ownership control to earning status as "large-scale business institutions, operating within the framework of the national business structure. Thus institutionalized, it was rapidly taking on the characteristics of institutions, becoming by and large a conservative defender of the status quo, although professing independence and progressivism."[247]

But what was lost in this transformation? While historians agree that newspapers in the early 20th century contributed substantially to political, social and cultural change, the newspaper itself had become a commodity. This is highlighted in the following editorial, published in

---

244   Mott, pp. 436–439.
245   Ibid, pp. 538–539.
246   John Tebbel, *The Compact History of the American Newspaper* (New & Revised Ed.) (New York: Hawthorn Books, Inc., 1969), p. 209.
247   Tebbel, p. 228.

The Nation in 1912.

. . .

Newspapers as Commodities
The Nation[248]

A writer in the *University Magazine*, who announces himself as a newspaper man, opens his heart upon the subject of "Why Newspapers are Unreadable." This is the last charge that we should have thought could have been brought against them, but apparently the word is used in the article as meaning not "refined." In this sense, there must be admitted to be point in its title. To understand why newspapers are unreadable, we are told that it is first necessary to consider the case of the maker of cheese. The cheese man differs from his university mates who have become physicians or clergymen or pharmacists or teachers. They received special training for their work, and possess certain privileges which protect them in the exercise of their respective professions. While they are free to go into the business of making cheese, the humble cheese man is debarred from competing with them unless he goes through such a process of preparation as theirs. On the other hand, they have obligations which do not burden him. The physician must rise from his bed at three o'clock in the morning if a human being is in peril of death; the clergyman undertakes to live a life of such godliness as shall convince all beholders that he is sustained by a more than human power; the pharmacist is bound not to take advantage of the ignorance of a patron – or, at all events, such advantage as shall be perceivably injurious to him; and even the teacher is strictly limited in the amount and kind of punishment which he may inflict upon the most unruly of his pupils.

The cheese man is troubled by none of these things. As cheese man, he owes no duty to the community beyond that of selling to it the sort of cheese that it likes, and this is not a legal but only a moral obligation.

---

248   "Newspapers as Commodities," *The Nation* (May 9, 1912).

Furthermore, it is one of those convenient obligations the observance of which benefits the one bound by it. He must, to be sure, obey the law, but what of that? Like the arrogant Trust magnate, he may, if he desires, engage the statute-book in a legitimate boxing-match, and even win some grudging admiration if he catches his opponent off his guard and scores a point. All that is really demanded of him is that he shall shake hands with the law before and after each bout. Now, the newspaper man, it appears, is not like the physician or the clergyman, but resembles the cheese man. Both discover as speedily as they can what flavor the public likes, and give it regardless of their own personal taste.

This particular newspaper man has found that the public likes its massacres in round thousands rather than in small and exact figures, that it is interested in religions only when they are fighting, that it has a passion for murders, and that it is utterly insensible to the monstrosity of the split infinitive. He has learned by the most convincing of all demonstrations – the sale of the product – that whereas readers want the truth about the price at which a neighbor has sold a lot, they prefer lurid romance concerning the reasons why Lord Haldane went to Germany; and, in a word, that they have no interest in international politics until they become bloody, none in art until it becomes scandalous, and none in philosophy under any circumstances whatever. "We have learned how to flavor the journalistic cheese," he declares roundly. "Shall we not do it?" But lest the minority that does not like its journalistic cheese so highly flavored should draw unwarranted conclusions from this frank disavowal of responsibility on the part of the newspaper cheese man, he hastens to explain that in practice the rule has the beautiful habit of tending in just the direction that this minority would desire. The cheese man, that is, who went to an extreme of coarseness in his flavoring merely because he found that the public was not fond of real delicacy, would be as foolish as his rival who made cheese that was not coarse enough. And in the end he would find it now only possible, but most expedient, to raise the taste of the consumers of his cheese. This is exactly what a newspaper does. It is dangerous for it to lower its standard for the sake of enlarging the circle of its readers, but it is the height of wisdom to retain its readers and imperceptibly elevate their tastes.

The difficulty with this theory is that it is too good to be true. Appetite is more likely to grow than to diminish by what it feeds on. Even the innocent cheese man, striving to give his customers what they want and at the same time make them want something else, has of late had to be put under pure-food regulations. Newspapers are exempt from analogous limitations, partly because of the difficulty of devising definitions of pure and impure reading matter, but more because of the deep-seated opposition to anything resembling a hampering of liberty of speech. To argue that the absence of such shackles is a sign and endorsement of newspaper irresponsibility is a strange reversal of logic. The moral responsibility of the press is great just because the fetters that once bound it have been struck off, and moral responsibility is worth while just because the press is and must be financially independent. An endowed newspaper would deserve no more praise for holding to lofty standards than a university student who had won a European fellowship would deserve for devoting himself to research work for a year. The problem and the opportunity of the journalistic cheese man is to provide a product that he can dispose of without selling his soul along with it.

·   ·   ·

Media Consolidation

Despite a growing population, the early 20th century saw trends toward concentration of media ownership strengthen significantly. Between 1910 and 1930, the U.S. population increased from 92 to 122 million people. Large cities grew even larger, and newspaper circulation across the country as a whole expanded from 22.5 to 40 million. Advertising revenue tripled between 1915 and 1929 – from $275 to $800 million. In 1910, daily newspapers had reached maximum diversity in ownership with 2,202 English-language dailies owned by 2,153 different people or organizations. Within 30 years, the number of owners had dropped to 1,619, about a 25 percent decline in diverse ownership. The cause was due to two trends – mergers and the growth of chain newspapers.[249]

Newspaper mergers came about mostly because of increased operating costs. The chain newspaper was born in Cleveland in 1887 when E.W. Scripps founded his first newspaper, the *Penny Press*. When the paper turned a profit, he and his brothers bought the St. Louis *Chronicle*, then the Cincinnati *Penny Paper* (which they renamed the Post). Scripps bought the papers to fight "power and privilege" and directed his newspapers to attack municipal and other forms of corruption. In 1887, after he split with his brother James, Scripps bought and expanded the *Detroit News* into a major newspaper. Soon after, he formed a partnership with Milton McRae, a businessman who took over the business operations of the newspapers. In 1907, the Scripps-McRae Association would join with two other news distribution agencies to form the United Press.[250]

By the 1920s, Scripps and Hearst had created important national newspaper chains. Scripps did this mostly because of his interest in challenging the status quo and taking on big business; the independently wealthy Hearst first became interested in newspapers while working at his father's *San Francisco Chronicle*. Over the years, he bought several newspapers and magazines and ran for a variety of elected offices, including serving in the House of Representatives in 1905 and 1909. Often, Hearst used his papers to promote his political causes, and historians agree that he exerted great influence over public opinion through his publications.[251] More chains emerged in subsequent decades, and as Oswald Garrison Villard notes in the article reprinted in this chapter, most of the people in a position to buy newspapers in the early and mid-20th century were either corporations or wealthy individuals.

Villard highlights the ultimate problem with mergers when he asks, "What is to be the hope for the advocates of new-born and unpopular reforms if they cannot have a press of their own, as the Abolitionists and

---

249   David Pearce Demers, *The Menace of the Corporate Newspaper: Fact or Fiction?* (Ames: Iowa State University Press, 1996), p. 46.
250   Tebbel, pp. 233–237.
251   Tebbel, p. 240; see also Kenneth Whyte, *The Uncrowned King* (Berkeley, Calif.: Counterpoint, 2009).

the founders of the Republican party set up theirs in a remarkably short
time, usually with poverty-stricken bank accounts?"

In addition to addressing the concerns raised by mergers and chain
ownership in the context of large city daily newspapers, Villard also mentions the problems created by the Western Newspaper Union's absorption
of the American Press Association (APA). As Villard explains, these
two companies supplied "boilerplate" news to thousands of rural, weekly
newspapers. The importance of rural papers in 1918 was underscored by
the recently passed postal zoning laws (as detailed in chapter five). These
papers, often called "country papers," flourished and reached a peak in
1914, when 14,500 weeklies existed in small, rural communities across
the country. Typically, these newspapers recorded births and deaths,
marriages, community social events and "happenings of everyday life."
They also published local news and political editorials.[252]

One of the best-known country editors was William Allen White, of
the Emporia *Gazette* in Kansas, whom Villard mentions in his article.
These small-town editors had enormous influence in their communities,
and while local news and happenings and opinions dominated their pages,
they also used material (articles and advertisements) from distributors
like the Western Newspaper Union.   Potentially, the "boilerplate" material that the Western Newspaper Union and the APA distributed reached
substantial numbers of people in communities across the country.

In 1912, a federal court intervened in a civil antitrust suit between
the two large corporations, noting that if a bitter trade war continued
between the two it would likely result in a takeover by the Western
Newspaper Union. The *New York Times* reported that this would result
in "the possibility of a combination to influence the thought of sixty million readers of rural newspapers."[253] While such a threat was staved off
in 1912, in 1917 the *New York Times* reported, "the Western Newspaper
Union had purchased the entire plate business" of the APA because "it
was unable to continue it on a profitable basis at present prices. The ener-

---

252   Tebbel, p. 255.
253   "News Trust Checked by Government Suit," *New York Times*, August 4,
1912.

gies of [the APA] will be devoted ... to the development of its advertising department."[254] The article makes no mention of the 1912 decision or any potential impact of the purchase.

Finally, Villard makes mention of a Supreme Court case pending when he wrote the following article. The case, *International News Service vs. Associated Press*, focused on unfair business practices and whether facts could be copyrighted. In the case, the Associated Press (AP) alleged that Hearst's for-profit International News Service (INS) was taking AP reports from the war and redistributing them as its own for profit. Often, the INS would get access to AP stories through bulletin boards or from early publication of an AP story in one or two newspapers. Some accounts suggested they bribed editors at papers to give them copies of AP stories before they were published.[255]

Ultimately, the Supreme Court agreed with the AP that this amounted to an unfair business practice, and rejected the idea put forth by Hearst that "the news is abandoned to the public for all purposes when published in the first newspaper." The Court further stated that the factual information in the AP stories was not copyrightable. In writing for the majority, Justice Mahlon Pitney said that by ruling in favor of the AP the court was not granting it "the right to monopolize either the gathering or the distribution of the news ... but only postponed participation by [AP's] competitor in the process of distribution and reproduction of news that it has not gathered, and only to the extent necessary to prevent that competitor from reaping the fruits of complainant's efforts and expenditure."[256]

· · ·

---

254   "Press Association Sells: Western Newspaper Union Acquires Plate Business of the American," *New York Times*, September 14, 1917.
255   *International News Service v. Associated Press*, 248 U.S. 215 (1918).
256   *International News Service v. Associated Press*, p. 241.

Press Tendencies and Dangers
Oswald Garrison Villard[257]

The passing of the Boston *Journal*, in the eighty-fourth year of its age, by merger with the Boston *Herald*, has rightly been characterized as a tragedy of journalism. Yet it is no more significant than the similar merger of the Cleveland *Plain Dealer* and the *Cleveland Leader*, or the New York *Press* and the New York *Sun*. All are in obedience to the drift toward consolidation, which has been as marked in journalism as in other spheres of business activity – for this is purely a business matter. True, in the cases of the *Sun* and the *Press* Mr. Munsey's controlling motive was probably the desire to obtain the Associated Press service for the *Sun*, which he could have secured in no other way. But Mr. Munsey was not blind to the advantages of combining the circulation of the *Press* and the *Sun*, and has profited by it.

It is quite possible that there will be further consolidations in New York as in Boston before long; at least, conditions are ripe for them. Chicago has now only four morning newspapers, including the *Staats-Zeitung*, but one of these has an uncertain future before it. The *Herald* of that city is the net result of amalgamations which wiped out successfully the *Record*, the *Times*, the *Chronicle*, and the *Inter-Ocean*. It is only a few years ago that the Boston *Traveler* and the *Evening Herald* were consolidated, and Baltimore, New Orleans, Portland (Oregon), and Philadelphia are other cities in which there has been a reduction in the number of dailies.

In the main it is correct to say that the decreasing number of newspapers in our larger American cities is due to the enormously increased cost of maintaining great dailies. This has been found to limit the number which a given advertising territory will support. It is a fact, too, that there are few other fields of enterprise in which so many unprofitable enterprises are maintained. There is one penny daily in New York which has not paid a cent to its owners in twenty years; during that time its income

---

257   Oswald Garrison Villard, "Press Tendencies and Dangers," *The Atlantic Monthly* (January 1919).

has met its expenses only once. Another of our New York dailies loses between four and five hundred thousand dollars a year, if well-founded report is correct, but the deficit is cheerfully met each year. It may be safely stated that scarcely half of our New York morning and evening newspapers return an adequate profit.

The most striking fact about the recent consolidations is that this leaves Cleveland with only one morning newspaper, the *Plain Dealer*. It is the sixth city in size in the United States, yet it has not appeared to be large enough to support both the *Plain Dealer* and the *Leader*, not even with the aid of what is called 'foreign,' or national, advertising, that is, advertising which originates outside of Cleveland. There are now many other cities in which the seeker after morning news is compelled to take it from one source only, whatever his political affiliations may be: in Indianapolis, from the *Star*; in Detroit, from the *Free Press*; in Toledo, from the *Times*; in Columbus, from the *State Journal*; in Scranton, from the *Republican*; in St. Paul, from the *Pioneer Press*; and in New Orleans from the *Times-Picayune*. This circumstance comes as a good deal of a shock to those who fancy that at least the chief political parties should have their representative dailies in each city – for that is the old American tradition.

Turning to the State of Michigan, we find that the development has gone even further, for here are some sizable cities with no morning newspaper and but one in the evening field. In fourteen cities whose population has more than doubled during the last twenty-five years the number of daily newspapers printed in the English language has shrunk from 42 to only 23. In nine of these fourteen cities there is not a single morning newspaper; they have but an evening newspaper apiece to give them the news of the world, unless they are content to receive their news by mail from distant cities. On Sunday they are better off, for there are seven Sunday newspapers in these towns.

In the five cities having more than one newspaper, there are six dailies that are thought to be unprofitable to their owners; and it is believed that within a short time the number of one-newspaper cities will grow to twelve, in which case Detroit and Grand Rapids will be the only cities with morning dailies. It is reported by competent witnesses that the one-newspaper towns are not only well content with this state of affairs, but that they actively resist any attempt to change the situation, the merchants in some cases banding together voluntarily to maintain the monopoly by refusing advertising to those wishing to start competition.

It is of course true that in the larger cities of the East there are other causes than the lack of advertising to account for the disappearance of certain newspapers. Many of them have deserved to perish because they were inefficiently managed or improperly edited. The Boston *Transcript* declares that the reason for the *Journal's* demise was lack 'of that single- ness and clearness of direction and purpose which alone establish confi- dence in and guarantee abiding support of a newspaper.' If some of the Hearst newspapers may be cited as examples of successful journals which have neither clearness nor honesty of purpose, it is not to be questioned that a newspaper with clear-cut, vigorous personalities behind it is far more likely to survive than one which does not have them.

But it does not help the situation to point out, as does the Columbia (S.C.) *State*, that 'sentiment and passion' have been responsible for the launching of many of the newspaper wrecks, for often sentiment and the righteous passion of indignation have been responsible for the foundation of notable newspapers such as the New York *Tribune*, whose financial success was, for a time at least, quite notable. It is the danger that newspaper conditions, because of the enormously increased costs and this tendency to monopoly, may prevent people who are actuated by passion and sentiment from founding newspapers that is causing many students of the situation much concern. What is to be the hope for the advocates of new-born and unpopular reforms if they cannot have a press of their own, as the Abolitionists and the founders of the Republican party set up theirs in a remarkably short time, usually with poverty-stricken bank accounts?

If no good American can read of cities having only one newspaper without concern, -- since democracy depends largely upon the presenting of both sides of every issue, -- it does not add any comfort to know that it would take millions to found a new paper, on a strictly business basis, in our largest cities. None but extremely wealthy men could undertake such a venture, -- precisely as the rejuvenated Chicago *Herald* has been financed by a group of the city's wealthiest magnates, -- and even then the success of the undertaking would be questionable if it were not possible to secure the Associated Press service for the newcomer.

The 'journal of protest,' it may be truthfully said, is to-day being confined, outside of the Socialistic press, to weeklies of varying types, of which the *Survey*, the *Public*, and the St. Louis *Mirror* are examples; and scores of them fall by the wayside. The large sums necessary to establish a journal of opinion are being demonstrated by the *New Republic*. Gone is the day when a *Liberator* can be founded with a couple of hundred dollars as capital. The struggle of the New York *Call* to keep alive, and that of some of our Jewish newspapers, are clear proof that conditions to-day make strongly against those who are fired by passion and sentiment to give a new and radical message to the world.

True, there is still opportunity in small towns for editorial courage and ability; William Allen White has demonstrated that. But in the small towns the increased costs due to the war are being felt as keenly as in the larger cities. *Ayer's Newspaper Directory* shows a steady shrinkage during the last three years in the weeklies, semi-weeklies, tri-weeklies, and semi-monthlies, there being 300 less in 1916 than in 1914. There lies before me a list of 76 dailies and weeklies over which the funeral rites have been held since January 1, 1917; to some of them the government has administered the *coup de grâce*. There are three Montreal journals among them, and a number of little German publications, together with the notorious *Appeal to Reason* and a couple of farm journals: twenty-one states are represented in the list, which is surely not complete.

Many dailies have sought to save themselves by increasing their price to two cents, as in Chicago, Pittsburgh, Buffalo, and Philadelphia, and everywhere there has been a raising of mail subscription and advertising rates in an effort to offset the enormous and persistent rise in the cost of paper and labor. It is indisputable, however, that if we are in for a long war, many of the weaker city dailies and the country dailies must go to the wall, just as there have been similar failures in every one of the warring nations of Europe.

Surveying the newspaper field as a whole, there has not been of late years a marked development of the tendency to group together a number of newspapers under one ownership in the manner of Northcliffe. Mr. Hearst, thanks be to fortune, has not added lately to his string; his group of *Examiners* and *Journals* and *Americans* is popularly believed not to be making any large sums of money for him, because the weaker members offset the earnings of the prosperous ones, and there is reputed to be great managerial waste. When Mr. Munsey buys another daily he usually sells an unprosperous one or adds another grave to his private and sizable newspaper cemetery. The Scripps-McRae Syndicate, comprising some 22 dailies, has not added to its number since 1911.

In Michigan the Booth Brothers control six clean, independent papers, which, for the local reasons given above, exercise a remarkable influence. The situation in that state shows clearly how comparatively easy it would be for rich business men, with selfish or partisan purpose, to dominate public opinion there and poison the public mind against anything they disliked. It is a situation to cause much uneasiness when one looks into the more distant future and considers the distrust of the press because of a far-reaching belief that the large city newspaper, being a several-million-dollar affair, must necessarily have managers in close alliance with other men in great business enterprises, -- the chamber of commerce, the merchants' association group, -- and therefore wholly detached from the aspirations of the plain people.

Those who feel thus will be disturbed by another remarkable consolidation in the field of newspaper-making -- the recent absorption of a large portion of the business of the American Press Association by the Western Newspaper Union. The latter now has an almost absolute monopoly in supplying 'plate' and 'ready-to-print' matter to the smaller daily newspapers and the country weeklies -- 'patent insides' is a more familiar term. The Western Newspaper Union to-day furnishes plate matter to nearly fourteen thousand newspapers -- a stupendous number. In 1912 a United States court in Chicago forbade this very consolidation as one in restraint of trade; to-day it permits it because the great rise in the cost of plate matter, from four to seventeen cents a pound, seems to necessitate the extinction of the old competition and the establishment of a monopoly.

The court was convinced that this field of newspaper enterprise will no longer support two rival concerns. An immense power which could be used to influence public opinion is thus placed in the hands of the officers of a money-making concern, for news matter is furnished as well as news photogravures.

Only the other day I heard of a boast that a laudatory article praising a certain astute Democratic politician had appeared in no less than 7000 publications of the Union's clients. Who can estimate the value of such an advertisement? Who can deny the power enormously to influence rural public opinion for better or for worse? Who can deny that the very innocent aspect of such a publication makes it a particularly easy, as well as effective, way of conducting propaganda for better or for worse? So far it has been to the advantage of both the associations to carry the propaganda matter of the great political parties, -- they deny any intentional propaganda of their own; but one cannot help wondering whether this will always be the case, and whether there is not danger that some day this tremendous power may be used in the interest of some privileged undertaking or some self-seeking politicians. At least, it would seem as if our lawmakers, already so critical of the press, might be tempted to declare the Union a public-service corporation and, therefore, bound to transmit all legitimate news offered to it.

In the strictly news-gathering field there is probably a decrease of competition at hand. The Allied governments abroad and our courts at home have struck a hard blow at the Hearst news-gathering concern, the International News Service, which has been excluded from England and her colonies, Italy and France, and has recently been convicted of news-stealing and falsification on the complaint of the Associated Press. The case is now pending on appeal in the Supreme Court, where the decision of the lower courts may be reversed. If, as a result of these proceedings, the association eventually goes out of business, it will be to the public advantage, that is, if honest, uncolored news is a desideratum. This will give to the Associated Press – the only press association which is altogether cooperative and makes no profit by the sale of its news – a monopoly in the morning field. If this lack of organized competition – it is daily competing with the special correspondents of all the great news-papers – has its drawbacks, it is certainly reassuring that throughout this unprecedented war the Associated Press has brought over an enormous volume of news with a minimum of just complaints as to the fidelity of that news – save that it is, of course, rigidly censored in every country, and particularly in passing through England. It has met vast problems with astounding success.

But, despite its many foreign correspondents, it is in considerable degree dependent upon foreign news agencies, like Reuters', the Havas agency in France, the Wolf Agency in Germany, and others, including the official Russian agency. Where these are not frankly official agencies, they are under the control of their governments and have frequently been used by them to mislead others, and particularly foreign nations, or to conceal the truth from their own subjects. As Dean Walter Williams, of the University of Missouri's School of Journalism, has lately pointed out, if there is one thing needed after this war it is the abolition of these official and semi-official agencies with their frequent stirring up of racial and international hatreds. A free press after the war is as badly needed as freedom of the seas and freedom from conscienceless Kaisers and autocrats.

At home, when the war is over, there is certain to be as relatively strik-ing a slant toward social reorganization, reform, and economic revolution as has taken place in Russia and is taking place in England as told by the London *Times*. When that day comes here, the deep smouldering distrust of our press will make itself felt. Our Fourth Estate is to have its day of overhauling and of being muckraked. The perfectly obvious hostility toward newspapers of the present Congress, as illustrated by its attempt to impose a direct and special tax upon them; its rigorous censorship in spite of the profession's protest of last spring; and the heavy additional postage taxes levied upon some classes of newspapers and magazines, goes far to prove this. But even more convincing is the dissatisfaction with the metropolitan press in every reform camp and among the plain people. It has grown tremendously because the masses are convinced, rightly or wrongly that the newspapers with heavy capital investments are a 'capitalistic' press and, therefore, opposed to their interests.

This feeling has grown all the more because so many hundreds of thousands who were opposed to our going to war, and are opposed to it now, still feel that their views – as opposed to those of the prosperous and intellectual classes – were not voiced in the press last winter. They know that their position to-day is being misrepresented as disloyal or pro-German by the bulk of the newspapers. In this situation many are turning to the Socialistic press as their one refuge. They, and multitudes who have gradually been losing faith in the reliability of our journalism, for one reason or another, can still be won back if we journalists will but slake our intense thirst for reliable, trustworthy news, for opinions free from class bias and not always set forth from the point of view of the well-to-do and the privileged. How to respond to this need is the greatest problem before the American press. Meanwhile, on the business side, we drift toward consolidation on a resistless economic current, which foams past numberless rocks, and leads no man knows whither.

.   .   .

Wartime Speech and Press Freedom, 1917–1919

Newspaper consolidation was not the only potential restriction on a wide flow of diverse sources of information to the public. As Villard notes in his previous article, many people who opposed the U.S. entering World War I were not able to voice their concerns and objections in the large daily newspapers. He wrote, "In this situation many are turning to the Socialistic press as their one refuge."

It may not be surprising, then, to find that socialists were one of the primary targets of new legislation aimed at stopping their perceived and potential impact on society and on U.S. politics during the war. Because socialists and other "radicals" were clearly the target, and because the U.S. had entered a period of extraordinary patriotism that led to a powerful marginalization of dissenting voices, much of the U.S. Congress did not object to the passage of new legislation that took aim at limiting activities that would aid the "enemy."

In June 1917, President Woodrow Wilson signed the Espionage Act into law. It held that when the U.S. is at war, no one can willfully cause or attempt to cause insubordination in the military; that people could not willfully obstruct recruiting; that people could not willfully make or convey false reports or false statements with the intent to interfere with the operations or success of the military or to promote the success of its enemies; and, that any printed material of any kind that is in violation of the Espionage Act provisions could not be mailed through the U.S. postal service.[258]

Historian Bob Mann notes that Congress removed a direct press censorship provision in the early versions of the law. He quotes Massachusetts Senator Henry Cabot Lodge from the May 11, 1917 *Congressional Record*, who said, "To attempt to deny to the press all legitimate criticism either of Congress or the Executive is going very dangerously far."[259] Lodge and other members of Congress believed they had removed all of the provisions from the law that would suppress free speech and press. But, they were mistaken.

In the few years after the passage of the Espionage Act, the Justice Department would prosecute 2,168 people under the law, convicting 1,055 for speaking against the war. Of those convicted, most were leaders of the socialist Industrial Workers of the World labor union (also known as Wobblies) or leaders in the Socialist Party.[260]

The U.S. Supreme Court would eventually determine the constitutionality of the Espionage Act in a series of cases it heard in 1919. First Amendment scholars point to this series of cases as a landmark in free speech and press jurisprudence, even if the results did not prove friendly to speech and press constitutional protections.

The first Espionage Act case involved Charles Schenck, the general secretary of the U.S. Socialist Party. In August 1917, Schenck was ac-

---

258   The Espionage Act of 1917, as cited in *Schenk v. United States*, 249 U.S. 47 (1919), 47.
259   Robert Mann, *Wartime Dissent in America: A History and Anthology* (New York: Palgrave Macmillan, 2010), p. 72.
260   Mann, p. 92; see also Harry N. Scheiber, *The Wilson Administration and Civil Liberties* (Ithaca, N.Y.: Cornell University Press, 1960), pp. 46–47.

cused of attempting to cause insubordination in the military and naval forces and of obstruction of military recruiting because his party printed and circulated a pamphlet to drafted men. Schenck was also charged with illegally using the U.S. Post Office to distribute the pamphlets. The pamphlet argued that the draft was unconstitutional because it violated the 13th Amendment (which abolished slavery and involuntary servitude), and that World War I was a capitalist war, being fought for the interests of Wall Street.[261]

The Supreme Court held that Schenk clearly violated the Espionage Act since the pamphlet's distribution had the intent of obstructing the draft. Justice Oliver Wendell Holmes, Jr., delivered the opinion for a unanimous court. He wrote that there were no First Amendment implications in the case; therefore, the court didn't consider whether or not the Espionage Act violated the First Amendment. The majority simply held that it was unconstitutional to use words in a way that creates a "clear and present danger" that Congress has a right to prevent.[262]

Justice Holmes wrote, "The most stringent protection of free speech would not protect a man in falsely shouting fire in a theater and causing panic ... the question in every case is whether the words are used in such circumstances and are of such a nature as to create a clear and present danger; that they will bring about the substantive evils that Congress has a right to prevent."[263]

A couple of weeks after deciding the *Schenck* case, the Supreme Court also issued decisions in two other Espionage Act cases—*Frohwerk v. U.S.* and *Debs v. U.S.* A unanimous court reinforced what it decided in the *Schenck* case – that there was no First Amendment problem in either case.[264]

Frohwerk was a German immigrant who published the Missouri *Zeitung*, a German-language newspaper that said it was a mistake to

---

261   *Schenk v. U.S.* (1919), pp. 249–251.
262   Ibid, p. 252.
263   Ibid.
264   *Frohwerk v. United States*, 249 U.S. 204 (1919); *Debs v. United States*, 249 U.S. 211 (1919).

send American troops to France because it would be outright murder;
that Germany had an "unconquerable" spirit; and, that the draft was
unconstitutional. He also argued that the war was an effort to "protect
the loans of Wall Street." Justice Holmes, writing again for the Court
and upholding Frohwerk's conviction, noted, "We think it necessary to
add to what has been said in *Schenk* ... that the First Amendment, while
prohibiting legislation against free speech as such cannot have been, and
obviously was not, intended to give immunity for every possible use of
language."[265]

The Supreme Court's decision in the Debs case perhaps garnered the
most public attention, because Eugene Debs was a prominent politician
and social leader. He served as a representative in the Indiana General
Assembly in 1884 as a Democrat. In the 1890s he became a champion
for labor, and was one of the founding members of the International Labor Union and the Industrial Workers of the World (the IWW). He ran
for president as the Socialist Party candidate in 1904, 1908, 1912 and
perhaps most memorably in 1920 from prison, after the Supreme Court
upheld his Espionage Act conviction.

Debs was charged under the Espionage Act for a speech he gave
in Canton, Ohio in 1918. He promoted the growth of socialism and he
praised several people who refused to register for the draft. He said that
he hated war: "I have been accused of obstructing the war. I admit it.
Gentlemen, I abhor war. I would oppose the war if I stood alone."[266] The
Supreme Court, again unanimous, held the Debs' speech intended to
obstruct recruiting and therefore violated the Espionage Act. As in the
earlier two cases, the court also dismissed the First Amendment claim.

About eight months after unanimously deciding the constitutionality
of the Espionage Act in Schenck, Frohwerk and Debs, the court heard one
final case that suggested that the law violated the First Amendment. The
primary difference in the outcome of this case was that the court was no
longer unanimous. Justices Holmes and Louis Brandeis dissented.[267] In

---

265   *Frohwerk v. U.S.*, p. 206.
266   *Debs v. U.S.*, p. 214.
267   For a detailed discussion about why Holmes and Brandeis may have

Abrams v. U.S., a majority of the Court said that Abrams and four other Russian immigrants whom they considered anarchists printed a circular called *Revolutionists Unite for Action.* The pamphlet called President Wilson a hypocrite and a coward, and called for the workers of the world to unite and put down the U.S. government and capitalism.[268]

According to the majority opinion, written by Justice John Clarke, the "plain purpose of their propaganda was to excite, at the supreme crisis of the war, disaffection, sedition, riots, and as they hoped, revolution, in this country for the purpose of embarrassing and if possible defeating the military plans of the Government in Europe."[269]

The dissent, written by Holmes and joined by Brandies, attempted to clarify when and how the government could suppress dangerous speech by reframing what "clear and present danger" meant. Although at the time the justices' dissent didn't mean anything for Abrams and his fellow immigrants who were imprisoned and fined for their ideas, Holmes and Brandeis' dissent did have an impact on First Amendment jurisprudence and thinking many decades later.

The dissent suggested that the United States could punish speech that produced or intended to produce a clear and imminent danger against the security of the country. "It is only the present danger of immediate evil or an intent to bring it about that warrants Congress in setting a limit to the expression of opinion where private rights are not concerned."[270] Holmes continued,

> But when men have realized that time has upset many fighting faiths, they may come to believe even more than they believe the very foundations of their own conduct that the ultimate good desired is better reached by free trade in ideas -- that the best test of truth is the power of the thought to get itself accepted in the competition of

---

changed their minds in the Abrams case, see David M. Rabban, *Free Speech in its Forgotten Years*, 1870–1920 (Cambridge: Cambridge University Press, 1999).

268   *Abrams v. United States*, 250 U.S. 616 (1919), p. 620.
269   Ibid, p. 623.
270   Ibid, p. 628.

the market and that truth is the only group upon which their wishes safely can be carried out. ... I think that we should be eternally vigilant against attempts to check the expression of opinions that we loathe and believe to be frought with death, unless they so imminently threaten immediate interference with the lawful and pressing purposes of the law that an immediate check is required to save the country. I wholly disagree with the argument of the Government that the First Amendment left the common law as to seditious libel in force.[271]

In addition to the arrests and prosecutions, censorship showed up in general postal practices during World War I. The Espionage Act gave the Postmaster General the authority to exclude publications from the mail that he thought violated the Espionage Act. Albert Burleson, the Postmaster General at the time, made it known that "every Socialist paper in the country was in danger of suppression" and that his solicitor also thought anything "pro-Germanism, pacifism or 'high-browism' were also objects of suppression."[272]

In the September 14, 1918 issue of *The Nation*, Villard carried an editorial that criticized the government's choice of Samuel Gompers, the American Federation of Labor President, to travel around Europe and report back on labor conditions there. Because of this editorial, Burleson banned the edition from the mail. Villard protested loudly, and eventually the Post Office told him that it would release the issue of the magazine if he removed the editorial. Villard refused and wrote letters of complaint to President Wilson's secretary and the Secretary of the Interior. At his

---

271   Ibid, p. 630. Seditious libel occurs when people criticize the government in a way that would bring it into hatred or contempt. The concept was a part of colonial American common law, and was enforced at varying times in the 19th century, well after the ratification of the First Amendment. Its use historically has been to silence government critics. Seditious libel was a crime. Although not really enforced in the 20th century, it wasn't until the U.S. Supreme Court decision in *New York Times v. Sullivan* 376 U.S. 254 (1964) that the court formally stated that seditious libel was not compatible with the First Amendment.
272   D. Joy Humes, *Oswald Garrison Villard, Liberal of the 1920's* (Syracuse, N.Y.: Syracuse University Press, 1960), p. 37.

next cabinet meeting, Wilson ordered that *The Nation* be released. In response to this, the Postmaster's solicitor issued a public statement that said that all newspapers in the country should refrain from reprinting the "seditious utterings" of *The Nation*.[273]

Villard's response to the solicitor was a strongly worded wire that could have been written by his famous abolitionist grandfather who also fought censorship of his unpopular views: "No seditious or treasonable utterance has ever appeared in The Nation or ever will. I resent the base libel on me personally, but I resent more deeply the infringement on the right to criticize policies of the government -- a right which is guaranteed by the constitution. How far this right can be limited by arbitrary action of executive officers is the whole issue between us and no other."[274] Villard's biographer, Michael Wreszin writes that Villard was privately happy that *The Nation* was censored, because it allowed him to show first-hand how freedom of the press was seriously eroding in the United States during the war.[275]

The editorial from *The Nation* that is republished below was most likely penned by Villard. It talks about the dangers of the Espionage Act about four months before its passage. It called the bill what it was – censorship. The law was subsequently used to stop the spread of anti-war sentiment, to spread fear of socialism[276] among the general population, and to suggest that criticism of the war amounted to an obstruction of military recruiting. The passage of the Espionage Act and the emergence of Wilson's Committee on Public Information (detailed in the next chapter) led to a time of notable suppression of dissent in the U.S. in the 20th century.

---

273   Humes, p. 38–39.
274   Ibid, p. 39.
275   Michael Wreszin, *Oswald Garrison Villard, Pacifist at War* (Bloomington, Ind.: Indiana University Press, 1965), pp. 97–99.
276   Many use the term "Red Scare" to describe the two distinct periods of anti-communism in the U.S. The first Red Scare came during World War I, when people feared a workers' revolution in the country. They also feared the growing influence of the U.S. Socialist party in national politics. Some of the Red Scare mentality is evidenced in the Supreme Court cases previously discussed.

.   .   .

Another Menace to the Press
The Nation[277]

When war is declared, it has been well said, the first casualties are
free press and free speech. In order that we may not be behind Europe
in this matter, the General Staff of the army has produced a Censorship
bill which is to be rushed through Congress, it hopes, the day upon which
war is declared. By it our military men might set up a censorship so
sweeping that there could readily be forbidden not only the publication of
news which might be of assistance to the enemy, but even the discussion of
any campaign or of the action of any general, unless the censor permitted
it. And they are beseeching Congress not to wait for the declaration of
war, but to do it now in order to avoid the "confusion and dissatisfaction"
which might be experienced if the "censorship *and control*" should have
to be set up after the declaration of war.

Censorship and *control*. It is the latter word that interests our General
Staff most. Of course, there must be some kind of suppression of news
in war – that is one of the evils which are unavoidable. We had a certain
censorship in the Civil War, not always effective, it is true, because, by
reason of its being a rebellion within a nation, it was never possible to
stop illicit communication between North and South, and because no determined effort to urge the press to be careful not to print matter of value
to the enemy was made. But in 1898 there was an effective censorship,
effective enough for any valid purpose, and there is an extremely effective
one in force at this hour. What newspaper reader knows where our fleet
is to-day or what measures are being taken by the navy to prepare for
war? The President is approving all measures laid before him relating
to defence, but who knows what they are?

With this kind of regulation every one will be content. Why is any

---

277   "Another Menace to the Press," *The Nation* (February 22, 1917).

more needed? Why should we need what was not considered during a four-year struggle for the existence of the Republic? The only reason is that our militarists desire it because they wish to control not merely the news, but the opinion of the country as well. It is true that this does not appear from the bill. It authorizes the President to issue a proclamation "prohibiting the publication of all news referring to the armed forces of the government or the means and measures that may be contemplated for the defence of the country, except when such publication shall have been duly authorized, and he may issue such regulations as may be necessary to render such prohibition effective." But the bill must be read together with the monograph issued in connection with the proposed bill by the General Staff of the army. In this there is indisputable evidence that the control of the press, and not merely the control of the news, is what is in the minds of the authors of the bill. Obviously, given this bill, with the drafting of the regulations left to the officers of the General Staff, it would be easy enough to control the editorial pages as well as the news columns. There is an excellent example of what has happened in the case of the British Defence of the Realm act, which is also a brief and inoffensive sounding statute, but under which many of the historic liberties of the Englishman have disappeared; this was not in the mind of Parliament when its assent was given to the measure. Its extension through regulations is what has done the mischief.

At the very beginning of this memorandum of the General Staff is this statement:

> The press, powerful in peace, may become more so in war. By its editorials and presentation of news it may sway the people for or against the war and thus stimulate recruiting and hearten and encourage the fighting forces in their work, or, by adverse criticism, may tend to destroy the efficiency of these agencies.

A little later it recurs to this subject in these words:

> By criticism of campaigns, the action of certain officers or exploit-

ing others, the people will be led to lose confidence in the army with the result that the moral support of the people is lost; they cry for and obtain new generals and new plans of campaign, not based on expert knowledge and thought, with a consequent lengthening of the war or even defeat.

It admits that the people ought to know something about the progress of their troops and their navy, and then it explains that the reconciling of these conflicting needs is the duty of the censorship. To give the army unlimited power over the press so that it might put an end to criticism of the general or campaign that the General Staff liked would be about as dangerous a thing as could possibly be done.

We all know what happened in 1870 when the Emperor Napoleon by his control of the press completely deceived the French Republic as to what was happening. Let us suppose that Gen. McClellan had had behind him a sympathetic General Staff when Lincoln found it necessary to remove him, and that, through its censorship, the General Staff had so controlled the opinion of the newspapers that Abraham Lincoln could not have had the necessary support of the press in his removal of McClellan and of the generals who succeeded him with such disastrous results to the Army of the Potomac. Doubtless, the kind of censorship the General Staff would not like would have prevented any criticism for fear it might have stopped recruiting and have weakened the faith of the people in a successful termination of the war.

Now, it will, of course, be said in some quarters that our American Staff is to be fully trusted; that it will not seek to control editorial opinion. But the minute you begin to interfere with freedom of public utterance you endanger the Republic; this is no less true in war time than in time of peace. It is perfectly conceivable that the fate of the country might hang upon a sharp press campaign to change the management of a war. Some of the profoundest students of our Civil War feel that Lincoln had more military genius than his generals, and that his good advice far more than offset his mistakes in interfering with military operations. But freedom to discuss the fate of the nation ought not to be abridged on any pretext.

England has shown this. She has permitted in the main free criticism of her generals and their strategy, as witness the press denunciations of military fallibility in Gallipoli, Mesopotamia, and Serbia. This outspokenness has doubtless saved the lives of many thousands of British soldiers whom military incapacity might also have sacrificed. Our own General Staff nowhere shows that it has the slightest appreciation of the duty of the press to interfere like this in order to prevent disaster.

Chapter 9

Propaganda & the Rise of Public Relations

The United States entered World War I on April 6, 1917. At the same time, President Woodrow Wilson created the Committee on Public Information (CPI), charged with winning over public support for the war effort. In U.S. history, this is considered a major milestone in the use of propaganda by the U.S. government. It also marks the beginning point at which mass communication scholars have examined the application and potential effects of propaganda on public opinion.

Propaganda as a concept dates back hundreds of years earlier. The term originates with the Catholic Church during the Reformation. The Church established the *Congregatio de propaganda fide* (Congregation for the Propagation of Faith) in 1622 to manage its struggle against the growing use of science to better understand the world. A principle figure caught in the struggle was Galileo, who argued that the Earth revolved around the sun, based on his scientific observations through a telescope. The Inquisition tried and convicted Galileo of heresy in 1633, and he was forced to renounce his view. Mass communication scholars Werner Severin and James Tankard suggest that the term propaganda may have picked up some of its negative connotations of being untruthful from the Galileo incident, in which the Church was forced to argue a position that was scientifically false.[278]

Many current definitions of propaganda used in the field of mass communication trace back to Harold Lasswell's classic book *Propaganda Technique In the World War*, published in 1927. Lasswell defined propaganda as "the control of opinion by significant symbols, or, to speak more

---

278   Werner J. Severin and James W. Tankard, Jr., *Communication Theories: Origins, Methods and Uses in the Mass Media* (3rd ed.) (New York: Longman, 1988).

concretely and less accurately, by stories, rumors, reports, pictures and other forms of social communication."[279] Ten years later, Lasswell altered the definition slightly and suggested, "propaganda in the broadest sense is the technique of influencing human action by the manipulation of representations. These representations may take spoken, written, pictorial or musical form."[280]

Lasswell's definitions were broad enough to include advertising and other forms of communication that some would call persuasion, so subsequent efforts to refine the term's definition tried to distinguish propaganda from other forms of communication. A modern dictionary defines propaganda as "the spreading of ideas, information or rumor for the purpose of helping or injuring an institution, a cause or a person" and "ideas, facts or allegations spread deliberately to further one's cause or to damage an opposing cause; *also*: a public action having such an effect."[281]

Most discussion and analysis of propaganda as it relates to the media and government comes from wartime. In 1927, Lasswell noted four main objectives of wartime propaganda – to mobilize hatred against the enemy, to demoralize the enemy, to preserve ally friendships, and to gain the cooperation of neutral parties. This is what the CPI did during World War I. According to historians, the CPI created an "all-pervasive system" of communication that would reach the American public every day. "The influence of the CPI was felt in the daily routines of Americans. In the workplace and on the streetcar and train, the worker would likely glance at CPI war posters and would often find in his or her pay envelope a pro-war flier." This was also a time when the CPI showed its war films in the movie houses across the country. These films "enjoyed blanket bookings and [audiences] probably would listen to one of the CPI's 75,000 official Four Minute Men speakers who delivered short talks to audiences based on weekly themes set in Washington."[282]

---

279   Harold Lasswell, *Propaganda Technique in the World War* (New York: Peter Smith, 1927), p. 9.
280   Lasswell, quoted in Severin and Tankard, p. 91.
281   Merriam-Webster's Online Dictionary, available at http://www.merriam-webster.com/dictionary/propaganda [accessed January 16, 2011].
282   J. Michael Sproule, *Propaganda and Democracy: The American Experi-*

The press was also greatly impacted by the CPI. Headed by former muckraking journalist George Creel, the CPI knew how to get its pro-war message published in the newspapers. Largely, newspapers depended heavily on the information supplied to them by the CPI. As historian Bob Mann notes: "Using two dozen war expositions in cities throughout the country, six thousand press releases, seventy-five million copies of prowar pamphlets, the committee's information and propaganda easily aroused the patriotic passions of journalists and their readers. While America's young men were enlisting – and being drafted – to fight in Europe, the CPI enlisted artists, writers, advertisers and educators in its campaign to sell the war and vilify the Germans."[283]

Throughout the later part of the 19th century, the relationship between government agencies and the press evolved. In 1889, the Department of Agriculture noted that it wanted the results of the department's efforts made publicly available. Because the Government Printing Office was overburdened, the Agriculture Secretary relied on newspapers to get the word out. He mailed them press releases, pamphlets, bulletins and other announcements from the Agriculture Department in an effort to inform the public.[284]

At the level of the president, it was William McKinley and Theodore Roosevelt who often receive credit for giving the press more routine information and access. In 1897, McKinley invited the press into the mansion and proclaimed his general availability. Upon assuming the presidency after McKinley was assassinated in 1901, Theodore Roosevelt went a step farther and reserved a separate room in the White House for the press corps. When the building was renovated a year later, he established permanent quarters for the press in the building. In a 1910

---

ence of Media and Mass Persuasion (Cambridge: Cambridge University Press, 1996), p. 11.

283   Robert Mann, Wartime Dissent in America: A History and Anthology (New York: Palgrave Macmillan, 2010), p. 72. See also Richard M. Perloff, Political Communication: Politics, Press and Public in America (New York: Routledge, 1997).

284   Timothy E. Cook, Governing With the News: The News Media as a Political Institution (Chicago: The University of Chicago Press, 1998).

speech, Roosevelt noted that "almost ... the most important profession is that of the newspaper man ... [They] are just as much public servants as are the men in the government service themselves."[285]

It wasn't Roosevelt who single-handedly created the public relations infrastructure that today is not only pervasive in the White House, but throughout all government agencies. That also happened in private industry in the late 19th century (and will be addressed in greater detail after the Wilhelm article republished below). It was the intersection of public relations, propaganda and the general use of publicity by public agencies and businesses in the early 20th century that led to the notion that public opinion could be influenced by the press and used to accomplish policy goals. [286]

At points during World War I, it was difficult for citizens and journalists to determine what was useful information instead of propaganda. In "The Failure of the Fourth Estate," Donald Wilhelm recognizes the danger to the public when press autonomy is compromised by concerted efforts to influence the news.

.   .   .

The Failure of the Fourth Estate
By Donald Wilhelm[287]

The press of the United States, thru no fault of its one thousand Washington correspondents, is falling down.

The Constitution of the United States provided that "Congress shall make no law abridging freedom of speech or of the press," but it did not provide for the safety and security of the press, against acts by agencies,

---

285   Roosevelt quoted in James E. Pollard, *Presidents and the Press* (New York: The Macmillan Co., 1947), p. 594; See also, Cook, pp. 47–48; George Juergens, *News from the White House: The Presidential-Press Relationship in the Progressive Era* (Chicago: University of Chicago Press, 1982), p. 66.
286   Cook, pp. 49–51.
287   Donald Wilhelm, "The Failure of the Fourth Estate," *Independent* (December 28, 1918).

of the Government and of private or public organizations, other than
Congress. It said, by implication, what is patent upon the least consideration, that the integrity and freedom of the means of communicating
intelligence, so that the people of this nation can exercise their will and
conscience intelligently, is essential to the welfare of the nation; it did not,
could not, a century ago, set up thoro-going means to the maintenance of
the integrity and freedom of the press, but it is becoming more and more
imperative that some such means be employed. The proof lies in many
national defeats, two of which are sufficient to demonstrate, past doubt,
that we shall do well to look closely at a menace which may thwart national
expression in this country as fatefully as it did in Germany. These two are
the coal closure and the aircraft crisis, neither of which disasters, in its
relation to the public thru the press, is, generally, in the least understood.

There was no real scarcity of coal, as was pointed out first by this
magazine, when the coal closure came as a rending shock to the nation last
year. There was no scarcity of coal, but there was an arrant and criminal
and unpatriotic scarcity of light on the conditions of the railroads charged
with the responsibility of transporting that coal. This scarcity of light
was due directly to press agents used as a kind of camouflage corps by a
small group of railroad executives who were making a desperate fight to
keep the railroads from being taken over by the Government. Conditions
on the roads got worse and worse; the very elements conspired against
them; until, at last, too late to avert the costly coal closure, the Garfield
order came and more than 150 ships whose cargoes were imperatively
needed by the Allies were freed. Then the President stepped in, forced
action, got the roads taken over. He was able intelligently to do that,
not because, in those fateful hours when he should have had the utmost
cooperation from the press, the press informed him that the roads must
be taken over, but in spite of the failure of the press to do any such thing.

The press agents who, unwittingly, no doubt, thwarted the will of the
nation in the case of the coal closure, tho used much by corporations and
individuals outside Government control, got their start in the Government itself. The earliest considerable press agency of which there is any
record available was that established by Gifford Pinchot, in the Roosevelt

Administration, to carry out the work of forest conservation. Mr. Pinchot was a pioneer Dollar-a-Year man who had learned, somehow – perhaps from Colonel Roosevelt – the tremendous power of publicity, with the result that he established a publicity bureau which, when perfected, proved to be an exemplar. The organization chart and charter of that bureau, which the writer studied, amply demonstrated how perfect a machine it was, one achieving such good results that other Departments and Bureaus followed suit, establishing bureaus of publicity, some of which, like that of the Department of Agriculture, were really desirable. In many cases "special agents" were designated, or the press agent was an "assistant," or an accountant, or a clerk. Congress did not give general cognizance to any such program in its appropriations. Perhaps Congressmen and Senators would have felt, in a test, sympathetic, because nearly every one of them relies, at least to some extent, upon the advice and guidance of a favored newspaperman, as indeed, the White House relies upon them all when it wishes to ascertain the opinion of the country on any act or appointment about to be made, by putting out intimations and watching results. The Government and its many agencies thus lopped off – and this is the important point – a certain area that rightfully belonged to the reporters.

Many private corporations took heed. It was natural for them to do so, in the first place because, as their units became larger and larger, the work of publicity had to be centralized and controlled by one agency. And it was natural, in the second place, as a means of self defense in the days when muckraking was the order of the day and in the ensuing days when the Sherman Anti-trust Law was trying to halter organizations that were or might be, for want of other legislation, about to run amuck. Hence we had another area of the reporters' field lopped off and more of them called to serve special interests. This tendency has been steadily going on, in some instances with the result that one publicity agent has been able to centralize the publicity of many corporations, in one organization of his own.

With this background in mind one can understand better the facts now about to be given for the first time about aircraft propaganda and the aircraft blundering and delay.

In June 1917, it will be remembered, there came the cry for aeroplanes. Aeroplanes, thousands of them! "It may be, in solemn truth," it was said in an article in this magazine, "that the war will have to be won in the air." This same article quoted, accurately, one of the members of the Aircraft Board, as saying:

> We can get under way at once. If there is one thing we Americans stand for, it is quantity. For Americans, when the designing and engineering work is done, output is easy. And this output will be swift and sure. We can get out forty thousand engines, twenty thousand planes, before spring. Give us the money and we can get that many by spring and increase the output steadily, but we can't do that if we don't start till months from now. We must start *now*. . . . But we haven't the money!

The Aircraft Board did not have the money. Sentiment had to be made for getting it. So the country was appealed to, thru the Fourth Estate. In short order, so readily did the spectacle of the American "Eagle" winning the war appeal to American imagination, Congressmen and Senators were fighting to have the honor of introducing bills that were no doubt as much favored universally as any bills in the history of Congress. In short order the appropriation bills providing the unprecedented sum of $640,000,000 were passed, and others followed.

The point to be noted here is that the Fourth Estate made this appeal when it had been formally appealed to. It aroused with almost automatic surety the imagination of the entire country, in the space of a very few weeks. How the Fourth Estate was thus united does not much matter. The simple point is that about sixty of the foremost magazine and newspaper publishers of the United States were told, by technical and executive men from the foreign missions and from the Aircraft Board, that the program was practicable, that they had a chance and a duty to do their bit, that, indeed, they, alone, could achieve the miracle. "Winning the war," they were told, "is up to you."

Forthwith the Fourth Estate did its bit. It accepted, as patriotic men would do, the presumption that if the appropriation were provided, victory would follow. It established that presumption throughout the land. That presumption existed continuously – until the whole aircraft problem seemed to crash to earth like a house of cards and investigations and readjustments had to follow – all of which meant such delay that American aviators, in quantity, with planes in plenty, lost their chance "to win the war."

There has never been such a clean-cut incontrovertible exhibition of the power of the Fourth Estate. It did in a trice an unheard-of thing that would have won, or hastened the winning of the war, if others concerned did their part as it did its part.

"Then," the question at once arises, "why was it that the Fourth Estate permitted the failure of the aircraft program?"

The answer is that the Fourth Estate met, whenever, wherever, it turned to inspect that program, the damning German and undemocratic sign, *Verboten*.

The reporters of the Committee on Public Information were little better off than the other one thousand reports working in one way or another with the press in Washington. It was patent that with a wartime program as vital as that of the aircraft program, and as hurried, it would not have been practicable for one thousand reporters to be turned loose in it. And the reporters of the committee had to take what was given to them – they had to take what the officials in charge of the program handed to them, which matter they wrote to best advantage, had corrected and revised by said officials, gave, in the form of mimeographed copies, from a common clearing house, to the press. It is patent that this method was neither unprecedented nor wholly undesirable. All this has, since this article was written, been proved by the Hughes investigation. In a word, in Governmental affairs – the people's affairs – as in its relation to the private corporations and private individual affairs, the Fourth Estate has been and is reduced to the plight of a kind of court of intermediate conjecture, with what results we see and probably will continue to see until the freedom of the press is restored or until the Government or special interests take it over entirely, or until some other decisive change is wrought.

There are other results of this manifold encroachment upon the prerogatives of the press, which come rather easily because reporters are an easy-going impersonal group. The best ethics and traditions of journalism intend them to be impersonal. That is, they learn from their earliest experiences that they are reporters – prophets who forthtell, as the word should be translated, not prophets who foretell. The first lesson the reporter learns is "When you think you've written something clever, kill it!" And he is never thru learning the futility of taking sides, because he is never thru witnessing struggles between sides. That is why, on one hand, one must look with regret upon a tendency of late becoming more and more apparent – that of turning the news columns of papers to selfish ends – and, on the other hand, continue to cling to our respect for newspapermen as a group. Their mental integrity is their pride, and a result of this is that their united judgment is better, it is frequently said by Washington officials, than that of any group of men whatever. They are scientists, not lyricists; they are cogs in a great and wonderful machine, not individuals who have special ideas to champion or to oppose. This character of trained reporters makes them careless of the limitations being placed upon the vital function that they perform.

There are many signs, only a few of which have been described here, that we are in a lull in which much of the Fourth Estate is groping. The radical press, which is certain to rise with the new might, since the war is over, is, for the nonce, smashed down under cover by both private interests and Government interests. On one hand many private interests steadily are encroaching upon the field of the Fourth Estate. On the other hand, as part of the governmental control of various industries, such as the railroad and the telegraph, the Government has been, and is, doing likewise. Special interests, by various means, are extending their control or possession of more and more daily, weekly and monthly publications – necessarily – if put to the test they say – in self defense, which is something that anyone who knows their point of view can easily appreciate.

But now comes peace! And tho the Government, during the war, "got behind" the power of the entire Fourth Estate by adding to the *Official*

Bulletin, its daily, a weekly newspaper, by utilizing also means of conveying information that have heretofore been neglected, that is, by sending out 10,000 Four-Minute Men to address audiences in motion picture theaters, by using the motion pictures, too, by printing and distributing pamphlets and books and using other means of reaching the people of this country – soon it will have abandoned most of these media. The balance of power, then, will fall to the remaining Most Powerful. The emergency, and the battle between sides, will be over, the powerful will have been stimulated, not weakened.

All this steady but sure alteration in the affairs of the Fourth Estate is of significance.

It may mean, conceivably, naught more than such a transition, such a unification of interests as is occurring all over the world, such, conceivably, as, looking backward, we shall anon rejoice at.

Nevertheless, it behooves us to note and to remember:

That this was a war for freedom.

That this war began in a "battle of the books," that it was begun by books, and won by books, and will have its full fruits reaped by books; that long before troops marched athwart the freedom of little estates, words, in orderly array, marched first – the children with the sword.

Washington, D. C.

•   •   •

The Rise of Public Relations

In an essay published in 1918, philosopher John Dewey lamented the menace of propaganda to public opinion. He wrote, "democracies are controlled through their opinions," and noted "that opinions are formed by the material upon which they feed, and that propaganda disguised as the distribution of news is the cheapest and most effective way of developing the required tone of public sentiment."[288]

---

288   John Dewey, "New Paternalism: Molding Public Opinion," cited in James E. Combs and Dan Nimmo, *The New Propaganda: The Dictatorship of*

While many people took note of governmental propagandistic efforts to influence public opinion during World War I, few seemed to recognize the influence of the public relations practitioners of the time who represented corporate interests.

Public relations was born at the turn of the 20th century. This was a time when corporate growth and a growing public of investors were mirrored by the growth of consumers. As noted in chapters three and five, advertisers were using newspapers and magazines to sell their products to mass audiences. The American public was increasingly developing as a consumer society, one that redefined the purpose of the average citizen. Historian Michael Schudson writes that public relations developed as "a profession which responded to, and helped shape, the public, newly defined as irrational, not reasoning; spectatorial, not participant; consuming, not productive. This had far-reaching impact on the ideology and daily social relations of American journalism."[289]

In his article "The Menace to Journalism," Roscoe C.E. Brown acknowledges that the railroad industry was one of the first to utilize and promote the growth of what today we would call public relations. In 1906, the Pennsylvania Railroad hired Ivy Lee who helped them handle a railroad accident. Typically, railroads tried to suppress information about accidents. Lee advised the railroad to invite reporters to the scene at the railroad's expense. Lee's efforts on behalf of the railroads were about "absolute frankness" and developing a relationship of openness and trust between the railroads and the newspapers. A former reporter, Lee had opened his public relations firm, Parker and Lee, in 1904. It was one of the first of its kind. The firm's motto was "Accuracy, Authenticity, Interest." According to Schudson, many newspapers were hostile to press agents and corporate publicity efforts at the time, but they accepted Lee because he never attempted to deceive the press.[290]

Palaver in Contemporary Politics (New York: Longman, 1993), p. 40; See also Alan Cywar, "John Dewey: Toward Domestic Reconstruction, 1915–1920," *Journal of the History of Ideas*, 30 (July – Sept., 1969), pp. 385–400.

289   Michael Schudson, *Discovering the News: A Social History of American Newspapers* (New York: Basic Books, 1978), pp. 133–34.

290   Ibid, p. 135.

Generally speaking, in the early 20th century all public relations efforts were equated with or labeled propaganda. The terms publicity, public relations and propaganda were used interchangeably. Publicists were usually called press agents. Lee didn't see anything wrong with propaganda, defining it as "the effort to propagate ideas," and arguing that propaganda provided important ideas and information. He suggested this was useful so long as the public knew the source of the information. Lee was very successful as a press agent, representing some of the largest companies and wealthiest men in the country, including Standard Oil's John D. Rockefeller, Bethlehem Steel, and meat-packing giant Armour & Company, in addition to the Pennsylvania Railroad.[291]

The number of public relations practitioners steadily grew between 1905 and 1920 – and journalists disliked them. They saw press agents not as the "purveyor" of news but rather the "creator" of news. Journalists also saw press agents as a threat to their value, and as people who hindered their ability to do their jobs. *New York World* editor Frank Cobb noted in 1919 that in New York City before the war there were 1,200 press agents. After the war, he wrote, "how many there are now I do not pretend to know. ... The great corporations have them, the banks have them, the railroads have them, all the organizations of business and of social and political activity have them, and they are the media through which the news comes."[292]

Historians suggest that most journalists viewed press agents with contempt in the years leading up to World War I, but that the effectiveness of war propaganda "directly influenced the wider growth of public relations" in the 1920s and the press' willingness to widely circulate war-related propaganda and journalists' willingness to work for governmental propaganda agencies opened the door for press agents to dramatically impact the news.[293]

---

291   Schudson, p. 135; see also Edward Bernays, *The Biography of an Idea: Memoirs of Public Relations Counsel* (New York: Simon and Schuster, 1965).
292   Cobb quoted in Schudson, p. 139.
293   Schudson, p. 141; see also Stuart Ewen, *PR! A Social History of Spin* (New York: Basic Books, 1996).

Analysis of the content in some newspapers by the late 1920s showed that as much as 50 to 60 percent of the stories were either ideas suggested by press agents or stories written directly from information provided by press agents.[294] Brown's column below highlights the real threat of public relations and press agents to journalism in 1921. Few editors or journalists at the time felt they could crack the stranglehold press agents had on the flow of information. Brown suggests in his article that the remedy is "nothing short of a rule: Exclude all 'publicity,' ... shut up the propaganda bureaus, stop the deluge of tainted news, and once more open the closed doors to the disinterested reporter."

· · ·

The Menace to Journalism
Roscoe C. E. Brown[295]

A new journalism is abroad in the land. To the reading public it is often indistinguishable from the old journalism. Like some of the parasitic fungi, whose spores penetrating the cells of their host change its substance to their own tissues, but in turn shape themselves into the outward form of the original plant, the new journalism has fastened upon the old, used it for its own purposes, and masked itself in the appearance of the independent and self-determining press. This parasite is propaganda. Its instrument of infection is the press agent. Its result is an organ of public opinion more or less completely, according to the extent of the process, transformed from an unbiased, or at least autonomous, expression to a suggested and not disinterested utterance.

Twenty-five years ago, the press agent was known to newspaper men as the genial distributor of circus tickets, and as the facile chronicler of the wonders of the jungle and the romances of the fat woman. He kept reporters apprized in gorgeous fashion of the coming of new plays and

---

294   Ibid.
295   Roscoe Brown, "The Menace to Journalism," *North American Review* (November, 1921).

took a kindly interest in recovering actresses' lost jewels. For the rest, he left the reporters to go their way unaided to get their news as best they could, and to present it with that approximation to truth that comes from the detached appraisement of conflicting statements and dug-out facts. He was the scarcely recognized poor-relation of the journalist.

To-day the press belongs to a numerous, well recognized and well paid profession. His handsomely furnished office is next door to that of the president of the great corporation; he is the consultant of the organizers of great philanthropies, the mouthpiece of political leaders, the window-dresser of government departments. He lays upon the desks of the leading newspapers every day enough copy to fill their pages, news, editorial and advertising, twice over. And he succeeds in getting enough of this printed to earn his salary to the satisfaction of his employer, to establish his own importance in the eyes of publicity seekers, and to color effectually the picture of American life and its supposedly spontaneous movements presented to the American people.

The press agent commands a higher salary, strictly measured by his success in circulating propaganda disguised as news, than he could obtain in the direct service of a newspaper. Consequently trained writers that are ready to forego the journalist's ideal and give their pens to the service not of society but of a patron's ends tend in increasing numbers to forsake the editorial room for the publicity office, to the impoverishment of newspaper staffs. Their systematic and extensive preparation of pre-digested news is in turn changing the conditions of news gathering. They stand guard at many sources of news, fending off the too keen inquirer and leaving the newspaper the choice of letting itself be spoon-fed or going empty. The inevitable result must be the decay of reporting in its more difficult and for public purposes most important aspects, the growth of a race of mere retailers of ready-made intelligence, and the turning of the newspapers more and more to distribution, less of news than of what somebody wishes to be considered news.

The war gave a great impetus to propaganda. Surrender to it by the newspapers was a form of patriotic service. Mr. Creel's mental treatment, his suggestions of what the American people, to help win the war, should

believe about fights with submarines or building airplanes, were faithfully
transmitted to them by a mobilized press. For that the press need not
apologize. Even public opinion must goosestep in a military movement,
though it may know it is being fooled. The creation of a certain state of
mind was as necessary as the equipping of an army, and the newspapers
did their part to create it, without inquiring too curiously behind official
statements. Nevertheless this meant an adjournment of the free play of
public opinion, and unfortunately it has not reconvened. Semi-official
propaganda claimed succession to the privileges of the official propaganda,
and too often obtained it. Organized movements of every sort, religious,
political, philanthropic, selfish, realized as never before the potentialities
of the press agent, and found the newspapers habituated to unbelievable
hospitality and frequently, it might seem, to unbelievable innocence. For
to an extent never before seen, at least since the dark era of the party
newspaper dependent on politicians in the first third of the nineteenth
century, the American press is taking things at second hand and allowing
artificially stimulated sentiment to appear as the expression of natural
public opinion.

Yet the war did not give birth to the era of the publicity agent. His
sway began when some of the railroads and other large corporations awoke
to the fact that unpopularity did not pay. Alexander J. Cassatt, if not the
discoverer of this truth, was one of the earliest of the railroad executives
to realize the consequences of the hostile feeling that was growing up
against corporations. He not only tried to persuade his fellow railroad
presidents to meet half way the demands for regulation, but also sought
to put their aims and methods in a favorable light before the people. One
of his earliest approaches was to a newspaper writer of distinction, who
declined what seemed to him a princely salary, not because he did not
sympathize with Mr. Cassatt's wish for better understanding between
business and the public, but because, for himself, he would have no client
but the public. Writers were found, however, who undertook to give newspapers information about corporation doings, and the old habits of silence
gave way to positive volubility – in one tone. The newspapers welcomed
this hospitality and were in turn hospitable; but before they realized it

they had opened the gate to a wooden horse. They allowed the press agent to gain control of whole fields of news. Whereas the reporter formerly could gain access to corporation heads, make his own inquiries, and ask questions that gave him insight even if unanswered, now these men will rarely see reporters and screen themselves behind prepared statements. In a business crisis or industrial dispute – for the labor unions have not been slow to adopt the new method – it is almost impossible to bring a joined issue before the court of public opinion, because statements that are not responsive are frequently all that can be obtained.

In the lobby of the National Press Club in Washington, according to the *Editor and Publisher*, there is a table much like a free-lunch counter. On it are displayed every day the mimeographed copies of the hand-out articles, official and unofficial, that the press agents hope will prove bait for the correspondents. With a paste-pot and a little rewriting a brave show of covering the Capital can be made. If that were all, it would not much matter. The conscientious and enterprising correspondent would show the difference between news and propaganda. But unfortunately the persons for whom the press agents work have learned that, if they stand on propaganda statements alone, and make no other, the newspapers will take them; and so they have shut the door on the independent investigator. Moreover, the press agents are clever enough to dress up for their own purposes matter that has real news interest, or seems to an editor to have when he sees it in a rival paper; and so the reporter, by the pressure of external circumstance and to meet the short-sighted demands of his own office, is driven to be the mere mouthpiece of biased statement. This has gone so far that Mr. Frank I. Cobb of the *New York World*, a practical editor by no means inclined to quixotic standards, declares that the newspapers are not meeting major problems and are not driving at the heart of things, but are "skimming the surface, and it is only now and then that a reporter gets under the skin of these great events."

Another sort of propaganda, not new but growing, is that which seeks free advertising. Sometimes it is plain puffery for commercial purposes. As often it is extensive free publicity for enterprises, good, bad and indifferent, from an Interchurch World Movement to the creation of a personality for a nonentity with political or social ambition. Against the advertising space-grafter the American Newspaper Publishers Association has been for some time making a campaign. The legitimate advertising men have found themselves more than once about to close a large contract when a press agent stepped in and persuaded the would-be advertiser that for a small sum advertising could be dressed up as news and circulated free to the limit of his desires. A few months ago a highly-colored story of the escape of a Turkish heiress from Constantinople filled columns of space in American newspapers, only to prove a piece of publicity for a motion picture. No paper that had not blunted its news instincts by the habitual acceptance of press-agent concoctions could have failed to scent a selfish purpose in such a tale. When a leading automobile company, after the annual shows in New York and Chicago, publicly boasts that "more than twenty thousand dollars' worth of free publicity in the news columns of the New York and Chicago newspapers was the proud record obtained" by its advertising division during the shows, it is no wonder that the publishers are aghast at their own fatuity in letting columns of advertising disguised as "human interest" stories pass their desks. When a publicity agent undertakes to raise a $10,000 charity fund on a $2,500 commission, and does it with the aid of $26,000 worth of free reading matter, the newspapers may well ask themselves who are really supporting the philanthropies.

Sometimes, it is true, the editor grows suspicious that he is being used; but then the propagandist is ready for him. No more revealing exhibition of his methods of creating a false appearance of spontaneous public sentiment can be found than appears in a letter of the National One Cent Postage Association that fell into the hands of the American Newspaper Publishers Association shortly before the war. It read:

> In conjunction with the prosecution of our campaign for one cent letter postage, we find we secure invaluable assistance from the newspapers by their publishing articles in regard to one cent letter postage.
>
> We also find that if we send these articles direct they are often disregarded, while if we secure some of our friends to send the articles

to them, the newspapers use them very promptly.

Because of this fact, we are asking the assistance of friends of the movement to secure publicity for our work. I am taking the liberty of enclosing herewith an article which I have had prepared, and in which I have had your name inserted, and would appreciate it very much if you would place this in the hands of one of your local newspapers.

Call up the city editor of your best paper, and the one most likely to use the article, and tell him to send a reporter around to your office, that you have a newspaper story for him. Don't tell him what the story is about, but simply request that the reporter call and see you. When the reporter does come tell him that to save him the trouble you have written the story out yourself. Then hand him the enclosed interview.

He will be glad to get it in this shape, and will doubtless use it in about the same manner in which it is written. This will advertise our movement wonderfully in your territory and should prove of great assistance to us in the creation of public sentiment in favor of one cent postage.

Surely, the editor needs to be as wise as the serpent and as cynical as Satan, if he is going to safeguard himself against propaganda and make his columns a chronicle of real happenings and a reflector of authentic, un-"accelerated" thought.

Shortly before the war, Mr. Cobb has said, the newspapers of New York took a census of the press agents who were regularly employed and regularly accredited, and found that there were about 1,200 of them. There are doubtless many more to-day, and they have, as he pointed out, seized control of many of the direct channels of news of business, social and political activity, and closed them, except as information is filtered through themselves. Great firms and corporations carry on publicity as a profession, and for a fee will contract to put upon the map of popular thought anything from a railroad rate campaign or a political programme to a prayer-meeting or a charity fund. The *Editor and Publisher* reports that in one day last year 189,350 words of "publicity matter" were received by the *Washington Herald*, which equals 24 newspaper pages. It came from religious and "uplift" organizations, political parties, government departments, and commercial and miscellaneous sources of every sort. This was an average day, and that paper was not exceptionally favored by the press agents. How much of this was used does not appear, but a great mass of such material is regularly used or it would not be prepared in ever increasing volume. The skilled newspaper reader can detect it in almost every paper he sees. Already the ulterior purpose behind what appears to be innocent news is frequently questioned. If the general body of readers shall be driven to share that suspicion, to look upon the newspaper record of life as artificial, and cease to find in it the mirror of their own thought and action, the old journalism will be dead and the new journalism will be bankrupt.

From one point of view all this is highly flattering to the press. It is a tribute to its power. When bank and factory, church and college, official and reformer, all systematically scheme to make the press present their interest and their version of news, not as their own, but as its own, they acknowledge in act what they so often deny in speech, that the voice of the newspaper is really the voice of the community talking to itself.

No longer can even the greatest take the attitude of the Duke of Wellington, who, when the editor of a leading London journal asked permission to view the coronation procession of William IV from the roof of Apsley House, answered that it was of no possible interest to the Duke whether the editor saw the procession or not. The propagandist has this excuse for fastening himself as a parasite on the newspapers: It is almost his only chance to reach the ear of power. When Bolingbroke employed Nicholas Amhurst as his press agent for warfare on Walpole, he had to reach only a small handful of men, who made the public opinion of England, and a small edition of a tiny sheet answered his purpose. Hamilton put the *Federalist* into the mind of America through a little paper of possibly 1,500 circulation. Anybody with the aid of a hand press could then publish a newspaper on substantially equal terms with anybody else. But all that is changed. Not only has the cost of producing anything that can possibly hold its place as a newspaper become enormous, but in a democratic society the public to be reached is so vast that nothing but the great established machinery of publicity is adequate to the task. The existing journals have a practical monopoly of public attention, and only through them can it be effectively arrested.

Of course it is easy and is much the fashion to lay the blame for the sway of propaganda upon some mysterious "system," to complain that some malevolent and super-intelligent group of men are with a common purpose seeking to control the press. But that is mere witch-hunting. It gets nowhere. The simple fact is that all movements dependent on mass sentiment must be organized. Propaganda is as old as society. Only it has come to a new intensity, dangerous to the public and to the press itself because of its parasitic nature. It has taken a leaf out of the book of business efficiency. No "system," no group, has deliberately set out to poison public opinion. The world in general, which means a great number of individuals, each seeking his own ends, has discovered the value of publicity in a democracy and has sought it with the practicality characteristic of the age. Everybody desiring access to the public mind has adopted the ideas of a commercial civilization to obtain it. The same business method inspires the bank's press agent and its cashier. The publicity bureau of a political party or a college endowment committee studies the psychology of the sales manager, adopts his slang, and starts out to "sell" an idea to the community. And it was not long ago that a great body of religious leaders also became enamored of business efficiency and dreamed that with a large bank account, a huge office force, expert administration and unlimited drafts on newspaper publicity, they could "sell" to the world the Sermon on the Mount, if not the Apostles' Creed.

Undoubtedly a great deal of the mass of "publicity matter" that is offered by parties in interest to the newspapers and accepted by them has news value, and deals with worthy enterprises entitled to notice. But that does not make the prevailing habit of opening newspaper columns to press agents' productions less dangerous. Indeed it makes it more dangerous. Propaganda must have news value, real or apparent, to gain publication and then win attention. Its news value, disguising its insidious purpose, is the tool needed to break into the public mind. And the insidious purpose is always there. Great corporations and organizers of campaigns do not pay large salaries to able men just to save the newspapers the expense of getting their own news, benevolent as their professions of "saving the reporters trouble may seem." What they want is free advertising, otherwise "publicity," for some scheme or opinion of their own, and the press agent's offering, either by distortion, suppression, unwarranted emphasis, or sheer invention, achieves not a judicial summing up of the facts, but an attorney's special plea for his client.

The press agent will say, perhaps with some truth, though probably no editor will admit it, that the newspaper has made him a necessity by failure of enterprise, by neglect to exploit really important matters outside of the day's concrete happenings, by an unfair attitude toward business enterprises, and by teaching public speakers that, no matter how worthwhile what they have to say may be, it will receive scant attention unless it is handed out in typewritten slips. However that may be, the newspapers certainly opened the door, taught the fabricators of propaganda their trade, fell into the habit of taking things at second hand, and are now in danger of being overwhelmed by the flood.

What is the remedy? Nothing but the absolute refusal to recognize the press agent, or to publish news that is not prepared by the editorial staff itself and its disinterested agents. Some of the leading publicity men themselves admit the present abuses and advise editors to verify more carefully press-agent offerings, and to exclude concealed advertising, or whatever seems to be unduly colored. But that does not go to the root of the evil. In many cases, especially with matter coming from a distance, verification is impossible, and the protection of advertising space against grafters, commercial or philanthropic, is not the chief concern of the public. If the newspapers want to give away thousands of dollars every week in free advertising, that is mainly their affair; though the community does have a right to read news as news and advertisements as advertisements, and not be fooled into reading one for the other. But nothing short of a rule: Exclude all "publicity," will shut up the propaganda bureaus, stop the deluge of tainted news, and once more open the closed doors to the disinterested reporter.

The essence of the mischief in propaganda is not its falsity in any particular case, but its origin. The essence of journalism is its autonomous

expression of itself as an interpreter of society. The editor who is entitled
to confidence, and who alone in the long run will get it, is he whose every
utterance is his own. Neither the accuracy of a journal's news nor the
justness of its opinions is half as important to society as certainty that
whatever it publishes is the result of its own independent outlook on the
world in the capacity of a public watchman. That is its profession; that
is its trust.

Unless the American press rescues itself from this growing tendency
to be the mouthpiece of extra-sanctum preparations of news and "accel-
erations" of sentiment, and by its own self-contained enterprise seeks
out everything that is important for men to know and presents it as ap-
praised and interpreted disinterestedly by itself, it will cease to be the
Fourth Estate. Its claim to that distinction and influence rests on its
performance of a public function, and it will not endure the abdication of
trusteeship and the loaning of the instruments of current intelligence to
the irresponsible agents of propaganda.

References

"4 Whites and 6 Negroes Dead, 70 Wounded In Springfield Race Riot; Militia In Control," *St. Louis Post-Dispatch*, Aug. 15, 1908.

Abrams v. United States, 250 U.S. 616 (1919).

Andrews, Wayne (Ed.). *The Autobiography of Theodore Roosevelt, Condensed from the Original Edition, Supplemented by Letters, Speeches, and Other Writings.* New York: Scribner's, 1958.

"Another Menace to the Press," *The Nation* (February 22, 1917).

Aucion, James. *The Evolution of American Investigative Journalism.* Columbia: University of Missouri Press, 2005.

Baker, Ray Stannard. *Woodrow Wilson: Life and Letters.* Garden City, N.Y.: Doubleday & Co., Inc., 1931, Vol. III.

Bernays, Edward. *The Biography of an Idea: Memoirs of Public Relations Counsel.* New York: Simon and Schuster, 1965.

"The Beginnings of The National Association for the Advancement of Colored People," *New Crisis*, 106 (January 1999): p. 75.

Brooks, Van W. *America's Coming-of-Age: By Van Wyck Brooks.* New York: The Viking Press, 1915.

Brown, Roscoe. "The Menace to Journalism," *North American Review* (November, 1921).

Campbell, W. Joseph. "Not Likely Sent: The Remington-Hearst 'Telegrams,'" in *Journalism and Mass Communication Quarterly* 77 (Summer 2000): pp. 405–422.

Cassimere, Ralph, Jr. "Flashback: 80 years ago the NAACP goes to court." *Crisis,* 102 (1995): p. 34.

Chalmers, David Mark. *The Social and Political Ideas of the Muckrakers.* New York: The Citadel Press, 1964.

Chambers, John Whiteclay II. *The Tyranny of Change: America in the Progressive Era, 1890–1920.* New Brunswick, N.J.: Rutgers University Press, 2000.

Chapman, Michael E. "Pro-Franco Anti-communism: Ellery Sedgwick and the *Atlantic Monthly,*" *Journal of Contemporary History* 41 (2006): pp. 641–662.

Colburn, David R. and George E. Pozzetta (Eds). *Reform and Reformers in the Progressive Era.* Westport, Conn.: Greenwood Press, 1983.

Combs, James E., and Dan Nimmo. *The New Propaganda: The Dictatorship of Palaver in Contemporary Politics.* New York: Longman, 1993.

Cook, Timothy E. *Governing With the News: The News Media as a Political Institution.* Chicago: The University of Chicago Press, 1998.

Cooke, Adam. "An Unpardonable Bit of Folly and Impertinence": Charles Francis Adams Jr., American Anti-Imperialists, and the Philippines," *New England Quarterly* 83 (June 2010): pp. 313–338.

Coward, John. M. and W. Joseph Campbell. *The Indian Wars & The Spanish-American War.* Westport, Conn.: Greenwood Press, 2005.

Cywar, Alan. "John Dewey: Toward Domestic Reconstruction, 1915–1920," *Journal of the History of Ideas*, 30 (July – Sept., 1969), pp. 385–400.

Debs v. United States, 249 U.S. 211 (1919).

Demers, David Pearce. *The Menace of the Corporate Newspaper: Fact or Fiction?* Ames, Iowa: Iowa State University Press, 1996.

DeNevi, Donald P., Helen M. Friend, and John Bookout. *Muckrakers and Robber Barons: The Classic Era, 1902–1912.* Danville, Calif.: Replica Books, 1973.

Dicken-Garcia, Hazel. *Journalistic Standards in Nineteenth-Century America*. Madison: University of Wisconsin Press, 1989.

Diner, Steven J. *A Very Different Age: Americans of the Progressive Era*. New York: Hill and Wang, 1998.

Eisenach, Eldon J. *The Lost Promise of Progressivism*. Lawrence, Kan.: University Press of Kansas, 1994.

Emery, Edwin, and Michael Emery. *The Press and America* (5th ed.). Englewood Cliffs, N.J.: Prentice-Hall, 1984.

Ewen, Stuart. *PR! A Social History of Spin*. New York: Basic Books, 1996.

Filler, Louis. *The Muckrakers*. University Park, Pa.: The Pennsylvania State University Press, 1976.

Frank, Glenn, "The Parliament of the People," *Century Magazine* (July, 1919).

Frohwerk v. United States, 249 U.S. 204 (1919).

Gannett, Lewis, "Villard's *Nation*," 171 *The Nation* (July 22, 1950): pp. 79–82.

Gould, Lewis L. *America in the Progressive Era, 1890–1914.* Harlow, England: Pearson Education, 2001.

Guinn v. United States, 238 U.S. 347 (1915).

Harrison, Harry P. *Culture Under Canvas: The Story of Tent Chautauqua.* New York: Hasting House Publishers, 1958.

Harrison, John M., and Harry H. Stein. *Muckraking: Past, Present and Future.* University Park, Pa: The Pennsylvania State University Press, 1973.

Hillquit, Morris. *Present-Day Socialism.* Chicago: The Socialist Party of the United States, 1920.

Howe, M.A. DeWolfe. *The Atlantic Monthly and Its Makers.* Boston: The Atlantic Monthly Press, 1919.

Howe, M.A. DeWolfe. *Portrait of an Independent: Moorfield Storey 1845–1929.* Boston: Houghton Mifflin, 1932.

Houghton v. Payne, 194 U.S. 88 (1904).

Humes, D. Joy. *Oswald Garrison Villard, Liberal of the 1920's.* Syracuse, N.Y: Syracuse University Press, 1960.

Huntington, Tom. "THE MAGAZINE WORLD," 44 *Civil War Times* (2005): pp. 16–59.

International News Service v. Associated Press, 248 U.S. 215 (1918).

Jensen, Robert. *Citizens of the Empire: The Struggle to Claim our Humanity.* San Francisco: City Lights Books, 2004.

Juergens, George. *News from the White House: The Presidential-Press Relationship in the Progressive Era.* Chicago: University of Chicago Press, 1982.

Kielbowicz, Richard B. "Origins of the Second-Class Mail Category and the Business of Policymaking, 1863–1879,"*Journalism Monographs* (April 1986).

Kielbowicz, Richard B. *News in the Mail: The Press, Post Office and Public Information, 1700–1860s.* Westport, Conn.: Greenwood Press, 1989.

Kielbowicz, Richard B. "Postal Subsidies for the Press and the Business of Mass Culture, 1880–1920," *Business History Review* 64 (Autumn, 1990): pp. 451–488.

Kimball, Penn, The History of *The Nation*, According to the F.B.I.," *The Nation* (March 22, 1986): pp. 399–426.

Lasswell, Harold. *Propaganda Technique in the World War.* New York: Peter Smith, 1927.

Leonard, Thomas. *News for All, Americas Coming-of-Age with the Press.* New York: Oxford University Press, 1995.

Lloyd, Caro. *Henry Demarest Lloyd, 1847–1903, A Biography, V. 1.* New York: G.P. Putnam's 1912.

Mann, Robert. *Wartime Dissent in America: A History and Anthology.* New York: Palgrave Macmillan, 2010.

Marcaccio, Michael D. "Did a Business Conspiracy End Muckraking?" A Reexamination," *Historian* 47 (November 1984): pp. 58–71.

Marzolf, Marion Tuttle. *Civilizing Voices.* New York: Longman, 1991.

Mattson, Kevin. *Creating a Democratic Public: The Struggle for Urban Participatory Democracy During the Progressive Era.* State College, Pa., The Pennsylvania State University Press, 1998.

Merriam-Webster's Online Dictionary, available at http://www.merriam-webster.com/dictionary/propaganda [accessed January 16, 2011].

Miller, Stuart Creighton. *Benevolent Assimilation: The American Conquest of the Philippines, 1899-1903.* New Haven, Conn.: Yale University Press, 1982.

Miraldi, Robert. *Muckraking and Objectivity: Journalism's Colliding Traditions.* Westport, Conn.: Greenwood Press, 1990.

Miraldi, Robert. *The Pen is Mightier: The Muckraking Life of Charles Edward Russell.* New York, Palgrave MacMillan, 2003.

"Moorfield Storey, Leader of Bar, Dies," *New York Times (1923–Current file).* Oct 25, 1929, p. 27.

Morrison, Theodore. *Chautauqua: A Center for Education, Religion, and the Arts in America.* Chicago: The University of Chicago Press, 1974.

Mott, Frank Luther. *American Journalism, A History: 1690–1960* (3rd Ed.). New York:

The MacMillan Company, 1966.

Mowry, George E. *Theodore Roosevelt and the Progressive Movement* (Madison: University of Wisconsin Press, 1946.

Murray, Gilbert. *Liberality and Civilization*. London: George Allen, Ltd., 1938.

The Nation: An Alternative History 270 (Jan. 10, 2000): pp. 8–51.

New York Times v. Sullivan 376 U.S. 254 (1964).

"News Trust Checked by Government Suit," *New York Times*, August 4, 1912.

"Newspapers as Commodities," *The Nation* (May 9, 1912).

Northern Securities Co. v. United States, 193 U.S. 197 (1904).

Ovington, Mary White. *The Walls Came Tumbling Down*. New York, Schocken 1970.

"Pearson's Magazine," *New York Times*, Nov. 23, 1901.

Perloff, Richard M. *Political Communication: Politics, Press and Public in America*. New York: Routledge, 1997.

Peterson, Theodore. *Magazines in the Twentieth Century*. Urbana: University of Illinois Press, 1956.

"Platform of the American Anti-Imperialist League, 1899." Platform of the American Anti-Imperialist League, 1899 (January 8, 2009): 1.

Plessy v. Ferguson, 43 U.S. 537 (1896).

Pollard, James E. *Presidents and the Press.* New York: The Macmillan Co., 1947.

Pope, Daniel. *The Making of Modern Advertising.* New York: Basic Books, 1983.

"Postpone Zone Law, Publishers Urge: New York Association Says Radical Postal Changes will Disturb Business," *New York Times*, April 22, 1918.

"Press Association Sells: Western Newspaper Union Acquires Plate Business of the American," *New York Times*, September 14, 1917.

Procter, Ben. *William Randolph Hearst, The Early Years.* New York: Oxford University Press, 1998.

Rabban, David M. *Free Speech in its Forgotten Years*, 1870–1920. Cambridge: Cambridge University Press, 1999.

Root, Damon W. "The Part of Jefferson," *Reason* 39 (December 2007): pp. 34–39.

Russell, Charles Edward. *Lawless Wealth: The Origin of Some Great American Fortunes.* New York: B.W. Dodge & Company, 1908.

Russell, Charles Edward. *Stories of the Great Railroads.* Chicago: Charles H. Kerr & Co., 1912.

Russell, Charles Edward. *These Shifting Scenes.* New York: Hodder & Stoughton, George H. Doran, Co., 1914.

Russell, Charles Edward, "The Keeping of the Kept Press," 31 *Pearson's Magazine* (January, 1914).

Russell, Charles Edward. "How Business Controls News," 31 *Pearson's Magazine* (May, 1914).

Russell, Charles Edward. *The Story of Wendell Phillips: Soldier of the Common Good*. Chicago: C.H. Kerr & Co., 1914.

"Charles Edward Russell," *the Crisis* (September, 1941), p. 301.

Russell, Charles Edward. "Book Review: These Were my Forebears, *A Pioneer Editor in Early Iowa: A Sketch of the Life of Edward Russell*" (Washington, D.C.: Ransdell Inc., 1941), *The Crisis*, September 1941, p. 300.

Schneider, Mark. *Boston Confronts Jim Crow: 1890–1920*. Boston, Northeastern University Press, 1997.

Scheiber, Harry N. *The Wilson Administration and Civil Liberties*. Ithaca, N.Y.: Cornell University Press, 1960.

Schenk v. United States, 249 U.S. 47 (1919).

Schudson, Michael. *Discovering the News: A Social History of American Newspapers*. New York: Basic Books, 1978.

"Secretary Root Attacked: Anti-Imperialists Issue Circular Blaming Him Alone for Alleged Philippine Atrocities," *New York Times*, Sept 26, 1902.

Sedgwick, Ellery. *The Atlantic Monthly, 1857–1909: Yankee Humanism at High Tide and Ebb*. Amherst: University of Massachusetts Press, 1994.

Semonche, John E. *Charting the Future: The Supreme Court Responds to a Changing Society, 1890–1920*. Westport, Conn.: Greenwood Press, 1978.

Senechal de la Roche, Roberta. *In Lincoln's Shadow: The 1908 Race Riot in Springfield, Illinois*. Carbondale, Ill.: Southern Illinois University Press, 1990.

Scrrin, Judith and William Serrin (Eds.). *Muckraking! The Journalism that Changed America*. New York: The New Press, 2002.

Severin, Werner J. and James W. Tankard, Jr. *Communication Theories: Origins, Methods and Uses in the Mass Media* (3rd ed.). New York: Longman, 1988.

Sinclair, Upton. *The Brass Check: A Study of American Journalism*. Pasadena Calif.: Upton Sinclair, 1920.

Sproule, J. Michael. *Propaganda and Democracy: The American Experience of Media and Mass Persuasion*. Cambridge: Cambridge University Press, 1996.

Storey, Moorfield (John T. Morse, ed.). *American Statesman*. Boston: Houghton, Mifflin and Company, 1900.

Storey, Moorfield. *The U.S. Conquest of the Philippines*. Freeport, N.Y.: Books for Libraries Press, 1926.

Storey, Moorfield, "The daily press," *The Atlantic Monthly* (January 1922).

Swanberg, W.A. *Citizen Hearst: A Biography of William Randolph Hearst*. New York: Charles Scribner's Sons, 1961.

Tebbel, John. *The Compact History of the American Newspaper* (New & Revised Ed.). New York: Hawthorn Books, Inc., 1969.

Tebbel, John William and Mary Ellen Zuckerman, *The Magazine in America, 1741–1990*. New York: Oxford University Press, 1991.

Tushnet, Mark V. *The NAACP's Legal Strategy Against Segregated Education, 1925–1950*. Chapel Hill: The University of North Carolina Press, 1987.

Tyler, Alice Felt. *Freedom's Ferment: Phases of American Social History to 1860*. Minneapolis: University of Minnesota Press, 1944.

U.S. v. E.C. Knight, 156 U.S. 1 (1895).

Villard, Henry. *Memoirs of Henry Villard, Journalist and Financier, 1835–1900* (2 vols). Boston: Houghton Mifflin and Co., 1904.

Villard, Oswald Garrison, "Press Tendencies and Dangers," *The Atlantic Monthly* (January 1919).

Villard, Oswald Garrison. *Fighting Years: Memoirs of a Liberal Editor.* New York: Harcourt, Brace & Co., 1939.

Villard, Oswald Garrison. *The Disappearing Daily, Some Chapters in American Newspaper Evolution.* New York: Alfred Knopf, 1944.

Whyte, Kenneth. *The Uncrowned King.* Berkeley, Calif.: Counterpoint, 2009.

Wilhelm, Donald. "The Failure of the Fourth Estate," *Independent* (December 28, 1918).

Wilson, Christopher. *The Labor of Words: Literary Professionalism in the Progressive Era.* Athens: University of Georgia Press, 1985.

Wreszin, Michael. *Oswald Garrison Villard, Pacifist at War.* Bloomington, Ind.: Indiana University Press, 1965.

Index

About the Authors

Amy Reynolds

Amy Reynolds is the Thomas O. and Darlene Ryder Distinguished Professor II and Associate Dean for Graduate Studies and Research in the Manship School of Mass Communication at Louisiana State University. Reynolds' research focuses on dissent and the First Amendment, First Amendment history, and media sociology, particularly in relationship to media coverage of breaking news and of terrorism. She has previously written/edited four books, and authored numerous book chapters and journal articles. Prior to joining the Manship School, Reynolds was associate dean for graduate studies at the Indiana University School of Journalism. She has served on the faculty at IU, the University of Oklahoma, and Miami University of Ohio. Her Ph.D. is from the University of Texas at Austin.

Gary R. Hicks

Gary R. Hicks is associate professor and chair of the Department of Mass Communications at Southern Illinois University Edwardsville. He received a Ph.D. in journalism from the University of Texas at Austin. His research focuses on media representations of – and their impact on – society's marginalized communities. He has done qualitative studies of media portrayals of lesbians and gay men and the disabled. His current research focuses on media portrayals of mental illness.

CPSIA information can be obtained at www.ICGtesting.com
Printed in the USA
BVOW011959181211

278673BV00001B/2/P